HOLY SH*T, I'M A GIFTED "MISFIT"!

THE YOUNG FOLX GUIDE TO UNLOCK YOUR SUPERPOWERS

J.J. KELLY, PSYD

Difference Press

Washington, DC, USA

Cover Design: Jennifer Stimson

Painting on Cover: Nathan Prebonick

Editing: Cory Hott

Headshot on Cover courtesy of: Melissa Schmidt at Icarian Photography

Headshot on About the Author page courtesy of: Seamus Vanecko Photography

CONTENTS

To the "docs" at UnorthoDocs, Inc. You are all so smart, sweet, interesting, talented, and totally badass. Your hard work is inspiring on multiple levels. Don't forget me when you take over the world. And don't ever forget to laugh. I love you all.

FUCK. FINALLY

W ell hey there, kiddo. Nice to finally meet you. I've been waiting a long time to talk to you. To kick off our relationship with the radical truth working with me requires, I'll go first and be honest with you: I wrote the parenting manual, *Holy Shit, My Kid Is Cutting!: The Complete Plan to Stop Self-Harm* because a colleague was stealing my ideas and making them their own – even to the point where they'd say my ideas to me in conversation, as if they thought of that shit. The cheek, as the Irish say. Narcissists are always pulling shit like that – testing the waters of their bullshit on you to see if you'll say anything, but that's another book. But educating your parents first worked out anyway. See, before I could come over and see to you and your struggles, I had to talk to your parents first. No, not 'cause they're more important – or even because I wanted to. Don't get me wrong; since they are currently in charge of your food/water, money, shelter, and emotional well-being (that last one less and less since you're growing up), it's important to make sure they've got their shit straight and are on board with the most effective and healthy plan to support you. But, all along, I wanted to talk to you. Working with you is my jam.

Havin' a tough go of things, are ya? Of course you are. High school blows. College is much better; that one is true, but what good does that do you when it's years away and weeks feel like a decade (I'm writing this during shelter-in-place, so I have a keen remembrance of how time can be oppressively slow)?

So, what's your particular flavor of high school shit to deal with? Are you not cool enough? Not enough friends and parties to go to? Not athletic enough, smart enough, or good enough? Or maybe yer on the other end of the spectrum – you're too something: too loud? too quiet? too shy? too obnoxious? too opinionated? Or even too smart? too fill-in-the-fuckin-blank. And maybe you're getting in fights with your parents or your friends. And maybe you sorta know what you want them to understand about you. And you know you're pissed, AGAIN, and they're not getting you – again. And you're either gonna burst into tears mid-argument, punch something, or hate yourself later tonight. And all this makes you feel like the fucked up one. God, it's all rigged so you can't win for losin'. I get the misery that comes with being misunderstood. I get it clinically, and I just get it.

Bottom line is, kid: the reason you feel like shit (and we'll get into the actual naming of emotions that go with that sentiment later) is:

1. High school sucks. That shit about it being the best years of your life is only said by people who peak in high school, which if you think about how long we live and how much we can do and learn in that time, is pretty sad.
2. Everybody's insecure and energetically "barfing" that insecurity all over everybody else, and turning on each other to try to make sure no one sees how scared they are... Yes, even the "popular" kids.
3. You have a ton of big thoughts and even bigger emotions, and nobody's tryin' to understand you 'cause nobody takes young people seriously.

The last one is the most important reason you're so unhappy right now. Are you listening, kiddo? 'Cause this is the shit right here: you are different, and you don't fit in.

Duh, right? Tell me something I don't know, Doc.

Well, if you already know that, then riddle me this, Einstein: why do you keep trying to fit in? Do you think that might be what's making you miserable?

More on that later, but let's cut right to the real shit. Most people are unhappy and everyone self-harms/self-medicates because of that. Why the hell do you think I wrote my first book about cutting? Because that's a self-medicating behavior that's fuckin' hard to ignore, so it opens the door to talking about all the ways we try to avoid our emotions. Okay, so you're not cutting. Are you video game or Netflix binging? Are you obsessing about likes (or not likes) on Insta? Do you pour all kinds of emo shit out on a Finsta? Do you smoke weed most nights? Oh, no, you just vape or take gummies instead, so it's cool, right (eye roll)? You may not drink, but have you stolen zanny bars from any adult?... - 'cause in my biz we call that "beer in a pill." So I'm not tryin' to call you out (which is a rarity in itself). I'm just sayin' that everybody self-medicates (and/or self-harms) and it's mostly 'cause they're tryin' to escape negative emotions. Negative emotions – while natural some of the time – often overwhelm folx who lack a feeling of contentment and connection with themselves and others.

So yeah, school sucks. People are mean to you . Maybe you're even being bullied at school or online. You don't talk to your parents about it 'cause they don't get it, and maybe even you don't totally get it.

You wish you had more friends and more cool shit to do on the weekends. And all you want is to be good enough, cool enough, or maybe just not feel like shit all the time.

Sorry, kid. I know it's fuckin hard some days to go to school, much less do homework. What if I told you it could be different? Better? Would you believe me? What if you were cool? What would that look like in your head? What if you had hella friends and tons of fun and funny shit going on? Parties, kick-backs, interests to dig into, like mixing music or painting, boxing or snowboarding, graphic design, or a start-up business even? There are so many opportunities out there you haven't even thought of yet, much less explored. I know it sounds impossible – even bat-shit. Or maybe I'm just another doctor trying to make money off of some book? Wise up, kid. Nobody makes money on books anymore. Stick around and see if I'm fulla shit. I dare ya.

2

DID IT, DO IT, DONE

Ugh. This is the chapter where I'm supposed to tell you why I, specifically, am the one you wanna listen to/work with. I hate that. I'm always like, "I know what the hell I'm doin' so if you wanna go dick around workin' with someone else who'll take yer money and won't improve your life, be my guest. Piss off, then. I'll be over here helping somebody who's brave, curious, and serious enough about activating themselves to change." Big surprise why I like workin' with folx in their teens and twenties so much, right? I'm a bigger pain in the ass then all of 'em put together.

Still here, huh? Brave kid. Nice. So, smart as you are, you gotta be asking yourself, "Why this person?" Shit, when I was in high school, the punk motto was,

"Don't trust anyone over thirty," so I know I wouldn't have. I'm probably a whole you older than thirty by now – meaning, I'm your whole lifetime older than thirty (Wow, that is a harsh muthafuckin' reality right there.) The thing is, though, not only do I remember high school in my head, but I also remember the feeling – the feelings. I don't think most "adults" do; not enough to validate and respect yours, anyway. Now I'm not sayin' I agree with everything a young adult says or does, I'm just sayin' I understand and can validate the urges you have and why the dark ones lead to self-destructive decisions and actions sometimes.

I think it's that willingness to hear you and see you that has helped me help hundreds of young people laugh more, have more fun, and enjoy more of life and themselves. Damn, if you only knew how low some kids were when we first met. Some were cutting and self-harming, others were doing drugs and/or drinking, others had had multiple suicide attempts and hospitalizations – even wilderness programs and therapeutic boarding schools. And damn-near all of 'em had problems with friends, didn't have any friends, constantly fought with their parents and even teachers – sometimes even the police. And every single one believed they didn't fit it – and that made 'em think they just would never be "good enough."

Now, these same young people have learned so

many tools for effectively managing heavy emotions and situations – including conflict. They're so skilled at this point that I'm even teaching them to teach the skills to folx younger than them. And they've even developed such a strong and grounded sense of self that when I have to crack down on 'em for destructive behaviors (yes, even skilled people still fuck up sometimes) they can face their fear and shame head-on and "eat a shit sandwich" with some dignity and move on. Yep. You bet yer ass I'm proud of these gifted "misfits," as we've come to call ourselves. Because you see, trying to be like everybody else instead of exploring and accepting who we are is the problem. There is so much in school and society and the world that needs to change. It needs to change; you don't need to fit in. It's fucked up. You struggling in a fucked-up environment makes sense. You haven't been encouraged to find out what your unique gifts are yet. Instead, you flail around in unhappiness and the destructive behaviors that come with misery. And if you've gotten to a dark place, that means you've put a ton of energy toward it; you'd have to in order to get that low. The crazy thing is, when you go exploring and looking for who you are, what you're about, what you want, and what your values and gifts are, all that energy can be harnessed and redirected in a healthy way. Yes, it can. And then there will be no stopping you. Then you'll soar. Then you'll have found your superpower and you'll have learned the skills to use it, in service to yourself and in service to the world. I've seen it before and we're gonna do it again – starting now.

3

TIME TO GET REAL

Whatever you're already doing isn't making you happy – can we agree on that? But let me just say – wait. Remember that climactic scene in the movie *Good Will Hunting* where Robin Williams (RIP) plays the shrink to troubled Matt Damon, and he has his file out and he says, "All this shit? It's not your fault," and Matt says, "Yeah, I know." And Robin's all, "No. No, you don't. It's not your fault." They go back and forth, and Robin keeps sayin' it, and Matt almost fights him until he finally breaks down crying and letting it out (by the way, it's a great scene for film, but I've never had it happen like that with folx I work with – I don't go pokin' the bear like that). So, let me just give you your *Good Will Hunting* hug and tell you: it's not your fault. All jokes aside, I mean it.

Don't get me wrong; I'm sure, by this point,

you've engaged in many behaviors that have caused you shame – and you chose that. It's just that you were in some kind of pain before you started engaging in those behaviors, and now you might be in a destructive habit or pattern. You may have even been an asshole – a bunch of times. Yes, the clean-up is your responsibility. It's on you. And I will help you with that. I just want you to know, deep into your guts and bones, that you didn't know what the healthy behaviors were – much less how to choose and enact them.

Yeah, you may have known the ones you were acting out weren't healthy, but I believe that if you had known what the healthy ones were, you may have chosen those. But who would've taught you those? Your parents probably taught you, some teachers, too. Treat others the way you wanna be treated. I think that if everyone just did that, the world would be a markedly better place.

But what about how we treat ourselves? We say shit to ourselves, in our heads, that is so vicious and cruel that we would never ever say it to someone else. We know better. Why is it okay to say it to ourselves?

"God, I'm so stupid."

"Why am I such a piece of shit?"

These horrifying statements are ones I've heard regularly when exploring with someone to find out what their inner monologue is like. What do you say to yourself when you make a mistake? What judgements? What does your inner voice say when you're embarrassed? Bet it's harsh. Would you say that same thing to your best friend? No way. Well aren't we first supposed to be our best friend in order to be a solid friend to others? But how? The four modules taught in this book will answer this question.

The good news is that if you're convinced you're the fucked up one you can use that 'I'm already the black sheep" shit to your advantage. You've probably already not met the expectations of others: parents, teachers, even peers. So, you've been exposed to what that feels like – not to please someone. You have learned to tolerate that reality to some extent. Great. Then when you have some skills to manage emotions and act according to your chosen values, when some people don't agree with that, you'll be ready. 'Cause even when you are healthy and happy and making effective choices, you can't please all the people all the time. So what? By then, you'll be confident enough to not care so much. And there is no need to take my word for it. You just need to decide you're going to apply a skill and when you experience the 'win' from using these tools then you'll have your data. That data – your data – will motivate you to bravely try another skill, and then another, and so it goes.

So here's what we're gonna do. We're gonna "Get Real." We'll get you some mindfulness skills in the first couple chapters so you can begin to notice and increase your awareness about what's actually important to you and what your emotional experiences are telling you. By chapters 7 and 8, we'll get you practical tools for managing crises and intense emotions. Once you have those skills under your belt, we can get you some assertiveness skills for interactions with other people. And then the later chapters will round out how to move forward in your newly developed emotional intelligence skillsets and find purpose and joy you can then share with the world.

4

GET GROUNDED

L ook, it's time we get real about what "mental health" means, looks like, and how it is enacted. What I teach works. I've seen the evidence hundreds, if not thousands of times. No shit. And I don't just teach it; I practice these skills myself. They are the tools I reach for to enjoy life and weather the times when the shit hits the fan.

It's not new information – and it's not "mine." In fact, what I named the "Get REAL" method is just my way of conveying old ideas. My "Get REAL" method is based on Dialectical Behavior Therapy (DBT), which was made by Dr. Marsha Linehan. She combined Zen Mindfulness Practices with Cognitive Behavior Therapy (CBT). The Zen Mindfulness Practices – two of the four modules of DBT – Linehan got from Thich Naht Hahn's book, *The Miracle of Mindfulness*, which is super old Buddhist tradition. So yeah, none of this stuff is original. I've had the pleasure of teaching these classes for more than fifteen years, and I've watched people change their lives, for the infinitely better, practicing these skills. So let's get into it.

I always start with some basic vocab, so I don't keep saying words that make no sense to you.

Dialectics (as in DBT, Dialectical Behavior Therapy) is just a fancy term for something that seems like a paradox – two seemingly opposing things existing at the same time in balanced harmony. My whole life has become the Venn Diagram – those two circles intersecting – which represents any dialectic: black/white, right/wrong, worthwhile/worthless, even Zen/CBT, rational/emotional, acceptance/change, but we'll get into that.)

Emotional Dysregulation, which I've also been calling Emotional Activation, is represented by Figure 1.

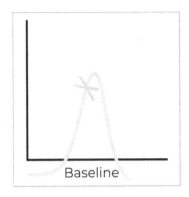

Baseline is you cruising along in life calmly. Then something happens, often called a "trigger" (not a fan because it kind of accuses or assigns "fault") or, in other words, an event that "activates" an emotion, and you're now off baseline in one direction or another. If you can then validate your emotion, in that moment, the validation alone can bring you closer to baseline – which can then allow you to mindfully apply your skills to bring you all the way to baseline before you make a decision about how you want to behave regarding that initial "trigger."

Validation is simply acknowledging (often just with an emotion word: happy, sad, angry, etcetera) an emotion we are experiencing. We validate all emotions, although not every thought that the emotion generates. When validating other people, we need not agree with them, simply acknowledge where they're at. "You look/seem pissed" is validating, even if you think their behavior is ridiculous.

Thoughts versus Feelings

This image is a simple diagram demonstrating a shrink-driven mistake that so many people make these days. Look at this sentence. Why is this ineffective communication? Well, for starters, "Like an asshole" is not a feeling. Feelings are emotions words – happy, sad, scared, mad, etcetera. Just because you say "I feel," doesn't make it a feeling. One tip-off is if you can replace the word "think" for the word "feel" in the sentence and it still works, that would make it a thought, not a feeling. So, "I think you're an asshole" works and is, therefore, a thought. Ya dig?

The next tip-off is the word "like" or "that" coming right after the word "feel;" that means you're on your way to expressing a thought, not a feeling. For your "I feel" statement to truly express a feeling or emotion, the next word after the word "feel" needs to be an emotion word or feeling, e.g., excited, surprised, ashamed, pissed, apprehensive, etcetera. The reason this way of languaging emotions is so important is because, remember, we validate all feelings, but not all thoughts.

Let's face it, we think all kinds of crazy shit – and that's totally okay. We're humans and we have imaginations, and we're lucky we do. We just don't wanna go through life believing every goddamn thing we think. Yikes. How truly terrifying. I often say to the folx I work with, "It's a nice place to visit, but you wouldn't wanna live here," while pointing to my head. As is my usual, I'm using humor to normalize the concept that dark, disturbing thoughts are had by everyone – even me, whom they look up to. It's perfectly natural and okay. No reason to deny the light and dark inside all of us. We can think whatever the hell comes in, we just don't want to act on every thought we have – or even believe every thought as a fact. So, we must develop an ability to effectively differentiate our thoughts from our emotions so we know which to validate – all feelings – so we can regulate them, but not all thoughts, and certainly not all behaviors based on those thoughts. That's how messes are made, and shame and regret are increased. Our whole goal is to reduce mood-dependent decision-making, because those are the impulsive and reactive behaviors that bite us in the ass later. I.e., "messes."

Acceptance/Change is the same as Validate/Problem-Solve Venn.

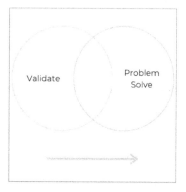

This is the one Venn that is not a true, balanced dialectic because it's linear. This is because validation must come before problem-solving. You must accept that there is a problem in order to change that problem. This is so easily illustrated when interacting with rookie shrinks (I use shrink to mean a psychologist and/or psychiatrist). So, you're in your shrink's office. You open up and say you're super stressed about an upcoming test and you just have to get an "A" or your parents'll freak. What do most mental health "providers" say next/first? "Well, have you studied?" "What did you do to prepare for the exam?" "You could do some breathing exercises before the exam." Swing and a miss. While these may be decent suggestions for problem-solving around your exam, somehow you don't feel any less stressed– like, at all. Why is that?

Well, basic DBT says that you weren't validated first. While "stressed" is kind of a catch-all – nonspecific explanation of how you feel about the test – quick questions could easily get you to a more specific feeling: probably something in the fear camp, right? But, even if you said a specific emotion word, "I'm scared about my test tomorrow," for instance, a simple validation statement could provide some relief. I might say, "Yikes. Is it in math again?" Or knowing me, I'd probably say something like, "Yeah, shit, you definitely look stressed out." We haven't even figured out what to do about the test yet, but you'll feel a little less fear just knowing I've met you where you are. It's the whole be-versus-do thing.

You feel seen, heard, understood (those aren't technically feelings, but you know what I mean – calmer). You now trust that I get it. And if you believe that I get you, you'll be calmer and more open to us proceeding to the problem-solving part of our show, dig? Plus, a calmer brain just works better – your frontal lobe isn't as activated, and you'll have better executive functioning (just to give you a lil' neurophysiology there, executive functioning is like the conductor of the orchestra where the instrument sections are memory, concentration, attention). Also, trust is established. You trust I'm interested in listening to you and understanding where you're coming from and I'm not just tryin' to be the answer queen.

I'm not saying shrinks don't care. In fact, I think many do care. There's just this control-mastery concept called intention versus impact, which basically says that regardless of what you intend to do (help), it may not always match with the way it lands for the other person: impact. "You just skipped the fact that I'm scared and now I feel invalidated." This happens a lot. And you can easily see how this could go down with parents, teachers, and even friends; they lead with the solution without acknowledging where you're at/how you feel, and now you wish you hadn't even brought it up. It's such a bummer – and basically, the whole premise behind the saying, "The road to hell is paved with good intentions."

Don't even get me started on how much it sucks when you point it out to someone and they're like, "Well, I didn't mean to…" Yeah, well you did, so…

So, that's class number one in a nutshell. Then, I give skills to practice during the week. I try not to say the word "homework" 'cause all of us have experienced how much homework can suck. But that's basically what it is, though it does not suck. Promise. Plus, it's easy. This first week, you can:

1. Go look at the description of DBT on my website, if you haven't already, drjjkelly.com.
2. Google and print out an "Emotion Words" list or wheel. You want a hard copy 'cause we're gonna be using it.
3. Ask yourself, "How am I feeling?" several times a day and do it without judging those feelings – just use your list or wheel. P.S. "Stupid" is not an emotion. It's a judgement – something with an evaluative quality: right/wrong, worthwhile/worthless, and we're gonna get you outta the habit of overusing judgements (more on that later).
4. Practice validating yourself, others, and others with whom you disagree.

See? Told you. Homework = no biggie.

In the next chapter, we'll get into the nuts and bolts of the Core Mindfulness Skills Module.

5

GET "WHAT" WE DO

These days, the word "mindfulness" has made its way into the mainstream – even if the *practice* of it still eludes people. What I teach is straight from Thich Naht Hahn, so we begin, as usual, with a Venn diagram of reasonable mind and emotion mind in a balanced integration – we use both.

Reasonable Mind

Emotion Mind

We are mostly using reasonable mind for planning, organizing, and problem-solving. We are more in our emotion mind when we discover our passions, are in love, and pursue these things seemingly against all odds. Both can be positive and both can be negative – as is the case in dialectics (and in life, I would argue). Dialectics and mindfulness encourages us to discard our impulse to see life in black and white, and I consider my job to be helping folx manage the fear of living in the "grey" or the unknown (and it's all grey, dude). There is a tendency for people to misperceive reasonable mind as the preferred "mind" to be in (thanks, the patriarchy), but using reason to overpower emotion is often what gets us into trouble in the first place. What gets stuffed eventually blows, from what I've witnessed.

No, instead, the balanced place – the place we strive to make decisions from – is called wise mind.

Wise mind is thought of as like our intuition or "gut;" that kind of knowing without analyzing. You ever just know something? Deep inside of you and in an instant? When I learned DBT, I was taught "wise mind is kind" – which is not to be confused with nice, polite, or pleasing. Kindness considers all that are involved. Sometimes the kindest thing to do is say "no," otherwise you may violate your values by saying "yes" when you don't mean it, but you're just scared to say no. That is not necessarily kind to you or the other person. I wouldn't want someone to say they want to go see a Fishbone show with me just 'cause they were worried I'd get mad at them if they said no. If they're pouting in the corner while I'm trying to enjoy one of my favorite bands, that's gonna distract me from fun and piss me off (not really, 'cause I'd just ignore 'em but you get my point, right?), So, acting from your wise mind means you are in alignment with your values.

Speaking of values, do you know what yours are? This is usually when people mind-fuck themselves and start to question what a value even is. You know what having values means – don't over-think it. Or do; I can't stop you. I usually just have people make a list – so make one. Don't think; just write. Whatever you write is great; trust me, we'll edit later. So, once you have your list, you'll probably find some overlap. I know I did. I do my values list every once in a while, and on this last one I had "honest" and "truth" because I just puke out the words the first go and don't worry about it. Though I can make an intellectual argument for why these both could stay on the list because of subtle, yet "important" differences, I went with "honesty" in the end, mostly because I like to end the exercise with my top five. You see how deep you can go? Don't bother yourself too much; it's ever-changing as the years go on. I just want you to have an idea of what you stand for and why "integrity" might be on the list, too – although I loathe when people say "I was 'out of my integrity'" – what a bunch of intellectualized horseshit. Cut the crap. You lied, dude, to that person and yourself. Face it. Face it like "courage" is on your list of values. 'Cause you can lie in the short-term, but you're gonna feel shame in the end because deep down in your gut (wise mind), you know the truth.

You now have another way to measure whether you are in wise mind – are you in alignment with your values? And the last thing worth mentioning now is that, when you are in your wise mind, you are cool with whatever outcome happens in any situation. Whaaat? You heard me: whatever happens, you'll deal. Now, that does not mean you have to like or approve of an outcome; you can even dislike it. It just means you accept it. And accepting that it happened is not the same as not wanting to or even taking action to change a situation. Are you thoroughly confused yet?

Here – remember the Venn from before of acceptance/change and validation/problem-solving?

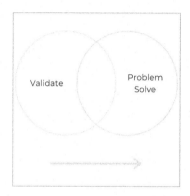

It's the one Venn I gave that is linear. As in, you must first accept that an outcome has happened in order to then change it. I accept that racism exists in the United States. Does that mean I'm okay with racism? Hell no. I fucking hate it. But if I don't accept that it exists and it affects Black folx in a real way, how can I change it? If I don't accept it, then there is nothing to change, ya dig? And though that appears to be the tack many white folx in this country have chosen to take, I prefer to use my undeniable white privilege to shine a light on racism in America in order to enact change. #BlackLivesMatterMuthafuckers

When it comes to acceptance and change, we

most effectively problem-solve in reality when we accept reality as it is, not attached and clinging to what we think it should be. "Should" doesn't help. You're welcome to have the opinion that racism should not exist – I'd not argue with that opinion – however, since it most certainly does exist, your "should" doesn't get us any closer to solving that problem, does it? You starting to get how this works? You roll your eyes now, but just wait until the next time you feel passionately angry about something in real life. Then, practice acceptance and tell me how "easy" it is and how I went over it too many times.

Now look back at Figure 4, at the "what" skills. This is easy to understand: observe, describe, and participate.

1. Observe is just to notice; an awareness
2. Describe is simply to put words to what you observed
3. Participate is to fully immerse yourself in what you're doing and in your life

We observe and describe in order to participate.

The goal of the "what" skills is to fully participate in your life, so we just keep observing and describing in order to participate. Sounds easy, and it is easy to understand. It's harder to remember to practice. So let's try an example. Let's stick with the math test example from before:

1. "I have a math test tomorrow," is your observe and describe of your current reality.
2. Now you make a choice from your wise mind (including your values): what do you want to do about it? I.E., how you want to participate in that reality. What is your most effective move? Study? Blow it off?

Now let's include emotions in this example

1. "I'm scared about my math test tomorrow," is your observe and describe. You didn't deny reality, even though I assume you don't particularly *like* the fact that you have a test tomorrow – nor do I assume you *like* your experience of fear about the math test.
2. With this acceptance of reality, you can now make a choice from your wise mind values about how you want to Participate

in the reality of your test tomorrow. Study
or blow off studying?

You can see from this example how this can
easily play out ineffectively if you deny your reality
or your feelings, right? You pretend (or "forget") that
you don't have a test and dick around all night
distracting yourself from your fear. You don't study,
you barely sleep, and you fail the test. So the core
mindfulness skills help us to know ourselves better
and learn what choices we want to make – and I did
say "want." You can tell yourself you have to study,
but is that the truth? You don't have to. You could
blow off studying and accept the consequences that
follow. Oh, no? Your parents would "kill" you? The
rare chance that your parent(s) follows through on
one of the many urges they have to wring your neck
aside, you most likely will not die.

Therefore, you still have a choice, and it seems to
me you want to choose to avoid the consequences of
failing your math test because you didn't study. I
guess you do want to study then because you want
to pass. Check and mate. Now look, I get that homework sucks, and tests suck, studying can suck, math
sucks, and you can blame your parents and blame
your teachers and blame me for now.

Pre-eighteen does seem like a whole lotta "have-
tos." And post-eighteen, dude, less and less people
to blame without just looking like a douche. I've had

pa-lenty of folx in their thirties and older come in still talking about so-n-so "made me" do this or that – to which I usually say, "You want some cheese with that whine?" So you gotta learn to root out the "want" in the "have to" sooner or later, and I swear to Goddess that you'll feel more confident, grounded, and strong when you do. There's something particularly sweet about knowing you have power of choice in a shit situation. I know that seems impossible, and it's totally true.

Another dialectic: joy/pain. It takes courage and strength to face something scary and/or shitty with dignity, and there is a special sparkle you'll feel inside you when you do. It's called self-respect, and there's nothin' finer. Also, it allows for those times it does match your values to ditch something someone says you have to do and go enjoy yourself instead, and you don't mind eating your shit sandwich about it later. And you'll do it with dignity. Yer welcome.

So, a homework assignment I typically use here is:

1. Write down several instances from this week where you used observe and describe to fully participate in tasks or activities – use your emotion words list.

2. Since we use observe and describe to get into our wise mind, write down several times this week when you were in wise

mind. And how did you know you were in wise mind?

Now let's continue on to the other half of the core mindfulness skills. As is the motto for the state of Wisconsin: Forward.

6

GET "HOW" WE DO IT

Unlike the "what" skills, which are practiced in a one-two-three linear way, the "how" skills are practiced simultaneously. The "how" skills are practiced non-judgmentally, one-mindfully, and effectively.

Core Mindfulness Skills

Wise Mind

"What"	"How"
1.) Observe	1.) Non-judgmentally
2.) Describe	2.) One-mindfully
3.) Participate	3.) Effectively

NON-JUDGMENTALLY

Non-judgmentally assumes we observe and describe without an evaluative quality; no good/bad, right/wrong, worthwhile/worthless. Let the arguing begin. "What? You're telling me there's no right or wrong? Nobody's a 'bad' person? What about that prick, Justin, at school? What the hell is this hippie brainwashing?"

Alright, grab the reins there, Haus. I'm not instructing you to no longer discern what or whom you like or dislike, or to ignore behavior that violates your values, m'kay? I'm saying that the more specific we can be with our language, the more effective we can be in our daily lives. You are welcome to have your values and behaviors that match and don't match those values. You are welcome to have opinions, even strong ones that we disagree on. What we practice when we're practicing our core mindfulness skills is stating opinions as opinions rather than as fact. "I don't like Justin," gets no argument from me or mindfulness. We generally wouldn't name-call because that's probably not from wise mind – meaning, most people (when they're honest with themselves) don't value name-calling, although "I think he can act like a real prick sometimes" might. It's all up to your wise mind values.

By the way, not all of your values are going to be the opposite of your what your parents taught you. Some of them will match your parents' values, and that's okay. True freedom comes when your values are based on what is genuinely important to you –

not just opposing people you are angry with in a moment. Bottom line: this is a tough skill to practice and will take some time. It's easiest to start with taking this non-judgmental stance with yourself first. Observe your thoughts (usually we call 'em worry thoughts because most are based in fear) about yourself and catch the habit of judgement. "I'm so stupid," becomes, "I wish I hadn't done that." "I'm a bad person," we reframe to "I made a mistake and I'm embarrassed." You are becoming more specific in your languaging in order to more effectively participate in your life. This leads to a greater understanding of yourself and what your experiences of emotion are and what they're telling you, and will come in real handy later when we practice communicating with another person – which exponentially increases the chances of misunderstandings.

ONE-MINDFULLY

One-mindfully is the practice of doing one thing at a time. We focus our attention fully on the task at hand – whatever that is in this moment. Wash your hands. Play your game. Talk to your friend. Be present with whatever it is you're doing right now. One-mindfully can even be practiced with worrying. It is an old psych intervention to have people who have a lot of anxiety that interferes with their day to set aside a half-hour at the same time each day to do all their worrying. Sounds nuts, huh? Yeah, but when your whole day is filled, morning until night, with intrusive worry thoughts, it can be effective to set aside that time to one-mindfully worry. That way, most people can catch themselves worrying outside that half-hour and just coach themselves to worry later – during the scheduled time. That cuts down on the daily amount right there.

The second benefit to this intervention is that by the time the half-hour comes, most folx don't have a whole thirty minutes of worrying to do. They find that most of that shit just repeats every time they feel any fear, and when they've disciplined their mind to do it at the scheduled time, they run outta things to worry about in ten minutes and get bored with worrying. Kinda cool, huh? And it's not a trick. You can know everything about this intervention and it'll still work. Try it if you worry a lot.

The one argument I almost always get when teaching one-mindfully is, "Well, what about multi-tasking? I'm not supposed to do that now?" First of all, no one's making you do anything, so bag the victim-y stance, yeah? Secondly, when you think about it, multitasking is more of a switching task anyway. You kinda go from one thing to another even though there are several tasks in a certain timeframe. So how do you know if you're doing multitasking mindfully? In my opinion, two ways: first, are you becoming emotionally activated or dysregulated? Are you feeling more and more anxious or frustrated as you engage in your tasks? Then, you probably aren't in wise mind. Hey, if you're getting more and more excited and happy more power to you. You may well be in your wise mind. In that case, giddy up! If you're stressed, you may wanna slow down, breathe, and attend to one thing at a time. Secondly, how are the tasks going? If you're doing several things at once and all of 'em are kinda going to hell in a hand-basket, you might wanna check out if you're in wise mind.

EFFECTIVELY

Effectively is how we strive to do most everything in our lives. It's kinda like the "what" skill of partici-pate in that way. In fact, I'd say we practice all the core mindfulness in order to effectively participate in life. What is your objective: to be "right" (whatever "right" even is) or to be effective in meeting your objective that's based in your values and emotionally regulated, i.e., at your baseline, calm, content, at peace, free?

Choice. You choose. Is your behavior chosen for what's most effective for the environment as it is or as you think it "should" be? Sometimes, when you're in the lower power position: in class at school, in an argument with your parents, at a job, being "right" might get in the way of being effective, especially if your objective is to avoid negative consequences. Sometimes keeping your mouth shut is the most effective thing to do. It's taken me a long time to embrace that one – and some would argue I have plenty of learning yet to do in that camp. The difference between you and me lies in our values. Lots of times I have just taken the consequences because to not stand up to something or someone for something I believe in violates my values. You choose for you, and I choose for me. I drive really fast, for example. That's against the law, but doesn't violate my values. You might disagree, and that's perfectly okay. Also, driving fast can increase physical danger and cost money in tickets, so that would not be the most effective choice in most cases – though it also doesn't make it, by definition, "wrong."

The core mindfulness skills module teaches tools to slow down reactivity and impulsivity in order to facilitate your awareness of choice and how to behave most effectively to meet your objectives in a way that is in alignment with your values. We're reducing messes and erosion of self-esteem and building courage and self-confidence.

A "homework" assignment for this week, then, might be to:

- Pick a real-life situation when you were emotionally activated (dysregulated, triggered) and write down how you were still effective. If you were not effective, why not? What got in your way of being effective?

- Make your unedited list of values – you are only doing it "wrong" if you don't do it.

7

R – RIDE THE WAVE

In the beginning of every new module, we review the core mindfulness skills, since they are the backbone of every other coping tool we add to your toolbox. Take another gander, and while you do, think about this little call-and-response cheer/chant to put the whole reason we learn these skills into perspective:

Me: "What do we do?"

You: "Observe, describe, participate. "

Me: "How do we do it?"

You: "Non-judgmentally, one-mindfully, effectively. "

Well done.

This week, we move into the Distress Tolerance Skills module number two. The Distress Tolerance Skills teach you how to bear pain skillfully when you are not able to make things any better right away.

No one lives a "pain-free" life, y'know? Life has pain. I don't agree with the mistranslation that life is pain, but painful times are certainly gonna come and go. And when we experience painful emotions, sometimes the best we can do is to notice we are experiencing a painful emotion (observe and describe), and not judge ourselves or the situation causing the pain (non-judgmentally, effectively), and not make any decisions until we've gotten ourselves back to baseline – since mood-dependent decision-making often makes messes. We can't always do anything about the pain part – shit happens, right? But we can reduce our suffering – pain and the non-acceptance of pain. Distress tolerance skills help us feel the pain and not make it worse. I know, right? Sometimes things just are gonna suck.

Distress tolerance skills can be employed when you're so emotionally activated (dysregulated) that you're approaching a crisis point. In fact, the first section is dedicated to skills you can use when you're in a crisis. These crisis survival strategies are tools you can use to "ride the wave" of intense emotions until this, too, passes. The second section is the meat and potatoes of the Distress Tolerance Skills module and especially fun to teach. They are the four basic principles of accepting reality.

Remember the Venn Diagram for acceptance/change and Validation/Problem-Solving and how this is the one that we used linearly?

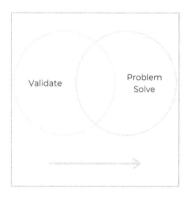

When you think of the four modules of DBT, think of the first two – Core Mindfulness Skills and Distress Tolerance Skills – as the first half: Acceptance and Validation. They're the Zen part. We must accept reality just as it is and validate our feelings in that reality before we can change it and problem-solve. Get it? It's important we learn these skills first so we can accurately assess our environment and the situation in this moment in order to maximize our effectiveness with how we then choose to act/behave in that situation. I know. The Zen stuff is hard. It's thousands of years old and super deep. I'm asking a lot of you, and I'll take you step-by-step, and you'll be happy you did these when we add the formulas for change in the last two modules – promise. Hang in there. Yer doin' great.

Okay, I'm going to run through the crisis survival strategies I teach, and feel free to make up your own in each category. I bet you already have some that have worked for you.

DISTRACTION

The skill of choosing to focus your mind elsewhere is one that, in my opinion, is overused in our culture, but shelving thoughts temporarily during a crisis can provide a rest for your central nervous system. Taking a walk, counting to ten while breathing, listening to your favorite song and dancing, playing a video game, or watching something funny on YouTube can give you a break from your distress – just keep it in moderation, please. We're not talkin' an entire season of something' on Netflix, ya dig? While you may know where that line is when you're not in crisis (and you may already cross it all the time – yikes), it can get blurred when you can't get yourself back into your wise mind. Set a timer on your phone. When I'm in distress, I go for something funny, and that laughing yoga cardiologist guy's worth checking out online, in my opinion.

SELF-SOOTHE

This set of skills deals with the five senses: vision, hearing, smell, taste, and touch. It's pretty self-explanatory from there and they can overlap as well. Watching funny stuff, as I mentioned, but also watching a fire or candle is super soothing (safety first, please). Watching or listening to water – the ocean, a river, even a shower – can settle things down a bit. You can see how water might be in the touch or even taste categories as well. Music and a bubble bath are winners for me. Lavender in a bath or diffuser or just oil on your wrist is surprisingly calming. You roll your eyes, but I'm serious – try it. While there are few things that a square of chocolate does not improve, you want to take it easy in the taste category, y'know? We tend to over-(and under)eat when we're stressed, and we go for sugar – which crashes later and can make you feel crummier. Just go slowly. Never underestimate the impact of a hug, by the way. Try a twenty-second one for the chemical (oxytocin) effect – you may even burst out laughing because of how awkwardly long that is. If you're alone, you can gently pat your heart and say, "There, there" to yourself. Yep. I know that one's weird, but I've come to enjoy it – plus crisis, dude.

Hello? What *won't* we try in order to end a crisis situation?!

IMPROVE THE MOMENT

This category is more the guided meditation kind. If you can picture yourself in your "happy place," as they say, or just a place you've been to that you found relaxing. I like the beach and the redwoods. If you pray, that would be in this category too. You can ask your higher power (or your wise mind) for help through this crisis. You can also use a mantra/affirmation – like coaching yourself into better times. You might say, "I can do this," over and over. I can picture a t-shirt I once saw with a cartoon cat on a train track with the train going over him while he totally freaks that said, "This too shall pass." God, as I write that it reads way more gnarly than it is in my mind. Sometimes it's the dark shit that sticks and comforts. What can I say? Yin 'n' yang, light and dark, whatever gets you through.

PROS AND CONS

This is just like it sounds. Write out both sides. Maybe pick the side with the most things listed. Maybe not. Either way, you just engaged your mind in a distraction skill exercise and probably got a little relief. It all counts in a crisis, as long as you didn't make it worse.

We also practice several breathing exercises, awareness exercises, and half-smile exercises where you relax your face and just gently turn up the corners of your mouth...Whatever works, right?

The four basic principles of accepting reality are different than the skills for surviving a crisis. These are so useful and important, I want you to understand them before moving on. That means if you need to read them a couple times or even look it up and get someone else's take in order to grasp it – do that.

RADICAL ACCEPTANCE

According to Dialectical Behavior Therapy (and The Miracle of Mindfulness) Radical Acceptance, supports the idea that fighting with reality almost always makes life worse instead of better. In fact, Thich Nhat Hahn goes so far as to separate the concepts of pain and suffering. Life has pain – it just does sometimes. That can't be helped, and it's not our fault either. I always thought there was some slight comfort in that – like a release of responsibility. I'm responsible for how I choose to behave when the pain comes, but I'm not in charge of making sure it never comes because sooner or later, it's here for a bit. That's life.

It's that idea and practice of releasing control. I can't control it not coming, only how I then act. Okay, that I think I can do. Without instruction, though, we don't even think of this practice: pain being inevitable and so let go of trying to control every aspect of it. We aren't taught to think that. No. What do we do? Well, we don't like the way pain feels: that is, painful emotions (we're not talking about physical pain right now) like fear, panic, sadness, grief, shame. We then avoid acknowledging it when we feel it and/or pretend we're not feeling it, maybe avoid taking risks that might cause those emotions, or just generally hide out from understanding our emotional experiences. We've all done it. Radical acceptance is the skill of not doing all that.

Accepting reality with radical acceptance is twofold. What makes this acceptance of reality "radical" is:

1. It has to come from deep within: that is, from your "wise mind." Remember wise mind from your core mindfulness skills? That middle place where the two circles of the Venn diagram overlap? Your gut? That's where radical acceptance lives.
2. It has to be complete. The complete part is also like the core mindfulness "what skill" of participate. Remember? We observe

(notice/become aware) and describe (put words to it) so that we can fully participate in our lives.

Well, radical acceptance helps free us from suffering because we stop fighting with reality. Wait. So what's the difference between the pain and suffering? Glad you asked. Someone always does. Well, the idea is that pain just happens, but suffering is our impulse to fight with, deny, deflect that pain, ya dig? Don't get pissy with me. The Buddhist shit is deep, dude.

Okay, let's try an example to break this down. Pick a person you know from school or your friend group that says mean things more than they don't. You know the person I'm talking about – everybody knows at least one. They've always gotta add their clever burn or tear-down when someone's celebrating something or happy or laughing. It's like it's their mission to shit on a good time (it's not, they're just debilitated by how much they hate themselves and fear being found out, but that's beside this particular point). You got the person in mind? Good. Okay, now just for fun, hold them in your mind and observe your thoughts and emotions about them in this moment. How does your body feel? Can you name your emotions (describe)? Can you find any tension in your body? Nice. You just completed a core mindfulness exercise and that's not even what I'm tryin' to do here.

Okay, so you've got this meanie in yer mind – let's call them Chris – and you've observed and described how you feel thinking about them: maybe tense in your stomach or shoulders, apprehensive, worried – mad, even. Now let's say something painful happens to you like, heaven forbid, your beloved pet dies. So you immediately text Chris, fully expecting them to comfort you. What? No you don't. Why the hell would you do that? Why would you go to someone known for unkind behavior for comfort when you're so low? You wouldn't 'cause yer a smart kid. But why? Because some part of you accepts the reality that Chris often behaves in an unkind way. Maybe you wish they wouldn't, but that's not up to you. You don't control Chris's behaviors. And you would cause yourself suffering on top of your pain of loss if you did not accept that Chris is not likely the person that's going to care about your feelings and support you. Is it becoming clear?

Now this is the *most important* point to remember about radical acceptance. Accepting reality is not the same as evaluating it as "good." You don't have to approve of or even like your reality at any given moment. In fact, you might hate it – and can hate it. Validate the hell outta your pain about your pet dying. Even validate your disappointment that Chris is too big a jerk to rely on in a painful moment. But fighting with the reality of either your pet being gone or Chris's unlikely support, and you're probably walking into a world of hurt – or "suffering" – by your own hand, because you chose to deny what's real. It's a powerful concept, radical acceptance, and the only way to get free. Might wanna read this section again. For real.

TURNING THE MIND

Okay, so "turning the mind" is the skill of the actual *choosing* to accept reality. Sounds simple, right? Well, it's not. I mean, it's a simple concept – simple to comprehend – but it can be difficult in practice, especially when emotions run high and it's most needed. Ain't that a bitch? This is tough stuff, kid. And to grab a line from *A League of Their Own* – that bitchin' movie about the professional women's baseball league that was formed when the men went off to World War II (which I totally would have played for if I had been alive then, FYI) – "It's the hard that makes it great." And you'll totally feel that pride the first time you succeed at this skill. Deadass.

Okay, so here's how turning the mind works: Picture a capital Y. In fact, picture me drawing a huge Y on a white board, 'cause that's how it goes down. Think of that Y as a road that starts at the bottom. You're cruising along and something happens. Now you're at what I call the "choicepoint," where the line splits into two roads. One road is the accepting reality road and one is the rejecting reality road.

Let's use an example. I love the driving examples, but so many young folx in cities don't drive. Let's say you're walking down the busiest street near you. You're on the sidewalk at a four-way stop. All have stop signs, so you walk into the intersection to cross the street. No biggie, right? Normal. Except the car that was rolling up to the stop sign on your right doesn't stop and the car whizzes past you, understandably scaring the crap outta you. Now you're at a choicepoint (I've been sayin' that word, choicepoint, for years. I thought I made it up in like, '05 but if it's somebody else's, don't sue me, 'k? Thanks). You may already know the "rejecting reality" road.

You may have been with friends a week ago and the same thing happened, and you all yelled, "Hey asshole, watch where the hell yer going," or other creative curse words like "asshat." And maybe that car started to make a U-turn and y'all scattered and ran and laughed about it later. Maybe the mouthin' off at a car is a well-worn path for you and you know exactly where it goes and even how it ends – and never to your liking. You may choose it again anyway – and we'll talk about willfulness in a minute – or you may turn your mind to a commitment to choose a new path. Choose a new behavior, chose a new outcome. The idea with turning the mind is that acceptance of reality starts with your commitment to choose the new way. It doesn't end there, though. Unfortunately, the commitment itself is not enough. I always tell people that a commitment to go to the gym is not the same as *going* to the gym. The commitment to the new choice is the first step, but it just points you down the new road – you still have to walk it. Plus, you might waffle and change your mind a buncha times, so turning the mind might need to happen hella times – even in the span of a few minutes. The flip-flop is real, my friend, especially when one of two particular emotions is on board. Can you guess which ones?

WILLFULNESS INTO WILLINGNESS

Ah, willfulness – one of my favorite concepts to teach. I like it because we all behave willfully sometimes, and sometimes it can be hard to choose to turn (the mind) that into willingness. I'm pretty sure Dr. Linehan, who created DBT, even says in the manual that we teachers of DBT should not give examples of ourselves "failing" to use the skills effectively. Yeah, fuck that. I'm a human being, and I also make mistakes. And I'm skilled at both practicing and teaching DBT effectively, and (there's that Venn diagram "both and" overlap) I spent most of my young life behaving willfully. I was always poppin' off to bosses, not doing what they requested. Yelling at unskilled drivers and tow truck companies. While I will say that telling the truth is one of my core values, age has given me some wisdom around how "truth" can be weaponized and hurt people – which is, by definition, not in wise mind because it's unkind.

I think it helps clients to admit mistakes and willful behaviors in that it validates how not being perfect is natural. Also willfulness is super funny. Talking in groups where there is trust and respect and active listening and love makes talking about all the ways we get in our own way hilarious and normalizing. Young people tend to idealize me in our work together, which is fine – to an extent – I'm a hell of a role model. But the observable relief I have seen in young people's eyes and posture when they hear shit I've done that was way worse than their behavior is worth it – in the right setting. Obviously, if someone is in the throes of cutting and suicidal behaviors, it's not funny – so I understand Linehan's point. Sometimes it can be validating to see someone you look up to laughing at themselves for mistakes and still have their dignity intact.

So what, exactly, is willfulness? I'm glad you asked. Willfulness is all the big and little behaviors we engage in that lead to us getting in our own way. And most of the time we know it. Willfulness is imposing one's will on reality. Look for the "shoulds," acting like someone should know better, a situation shouldn't be so hard/painful, etc. It often looks like paralysis when action is called for, but you've thrown in the towel. You're doing the total opposite of what you think would work. You've got yer head in the sand, or have your ears plugged while yelling, "La la la" while someone's trying to say something true and unappealing – even that image makes me laugh. I call it "rag dolling," because my first love's family taught it to me, and I did it to them all the time to be annoying. Rag dolling is letting your body go limp into someone. They will have the instinct to catch you/hold you up. They think you will take it from there, stand on your own two feet, and probably thank them for being a kind friend who caught you. Nope. You just stay limp and they continue to suffer trying to hold the dead-weight of your body up while you do nothing. If you truly want to annoy someone (and even maybe make them question whether they're a "good person" or not because they wanna drop you), look no further than this game. You're welcome. Yeah, that's will-fulness.

I heard this quote once about willfulness: "The bend in the road is not the end of the road unless you refuse to take the turn." Kinda circles back to turning the mind, right? You can think of that Y as the road that splits at the choicepoint, and the left road is the willful one – the well-worn road you know and have taken a million times. And the right side is the road of willingness, which is basically just doing whatever is needed in the situation as it is – not as you think it "should" be, remember? What does that sound like? The "how" skill of "effectively" from your core mindfulness skills, maybe? Yep. Willingness is something you do from your wise mind too. And that makes it a helluva great partner to radical acceptance, doesn't it?

I love teaching these four distress tolerance skills because it's so humanizing. All this Zen stuff is deep and simple and hard. But examples make them easier to understand. If only the understanding took care of everything, but it doesn't. It's the doing, the practicing of these skills – and all the DBT skills that bring these concepts into being. Practicing them makes them habit, and habit makes your life better. Consider this the beginning of your un-learning.

So this week's homework exercises are based on these:

1. Pick a situation from this week when you were emotionally activated (dysregulated) and try out something in the one of four categories of the Crisis Survival Strategies and write about your experience. (Note: you don't have to be 'in crisis', just pick a time where your emotions got kicked up and try one.)

2. Pick a time when you caught yourself

behaving willfully and write out how you changed it to willingness (or if you didn't, why not?). This one is kinda fun if you can laugh at how you were willful – we all do it. I find absurdity and hilarity in my willfulness.

8

E – EMOTIONAL BALANCE

Okay, those two modules – Core Mindfulness Skills and Distress Tolerance Skills – are the Zen Buddhist half of Dialectical Behavior Therapy (DBT) Skills Training. The next two modules are the Cognitive Behavior Therapy half of the course. And the Emotion Regulation Skills are next.

Remember: in the beginning of every new module, we review the Core Mindfulness Skills, since they are the backbone of every other coping tool we add to your toolbox. Take another gander, and while you do, think this little call and response cheer/chant to put the whole reason we learn these skills into perspective:

Me: "What do we do?"

You: "Observe, describe, participate. "

Me: "How do we do it?"

You: "Non-judgmentally, one-mindfully, effectively. "

Well done.

Dr. Linehan, in her wisdom, has beefed up this section quite a bit since I started teaching it, and it's worth checking out. I think it's way more user-friendly, so kudos to her. The core stuff's still in there, and we'll go over it all here.

First, the whole point of learning the emotion regulation skillset is to:

1. Understand our emotional experiences – which means we start to build our emotions vocabulary in order to validate our emotions – remember observe and describe. We also want to start to identify what currently gets in our way of reducing negative emotions.

2. Reduce our vulnerabilities to negative emotions as well as increase our positive

emotions, thus lowering our negative emotional sensitivity. See how that's kind of a loop there?

3. Decrease emotional suffering, which means that we want to choose to let go of painful emotions instead of walling them off, fighting with them, pretending we don't feel them (which you now know makes things worse instead of better, right?). I'm also gonna teach you a pro-move called "opposite action."

Okay, understanding your emotional experience is the only route to a calm, happy, fun life. I know, it's weird because so many people hide their emotions and have taught you to hide your emotions – even if that's not what they meant to do. A lot of people engage in behaviors that make them feel sad and mad and ashamed because they haven't been taught another way. More people go to therapy or a coach, but a lot of people still have negative judge-ments about damn-near anything having to do with emotions. I've got theories on that: that emotions are linked to the feminine, and we live in a patriar-chal society, so hell-to-the-no on the feels is one. But mostly I just think people are scared. Scared of what they feel. Scared to feel. Scared what it means to feel what they're feeling. Scared of other people's feel-ings. Scared of people they love expressing their feelings – positive *or* negative. Scared to slow down and know themselves. Scared to like themselves. It sounds weird... people having such an aversion to the science of human behavior. I always thought it made sense to learn all we could, y'know, 'cause we're humans.

Instead, what people do is react. They act in reaction to their emotions – instead of choosing their behaviors mindfully – which often means messes. Impulsive reactions to unregulated emotions almost always results in an outcome you didn't want... a mess. Then a person feels shame, but they don't know it's shame, and they don't know that most people hide from shame, so they bury it and now... another mess. Now, they've got buried shame just festering inside them, but they pretend that they don't and that makes them hella anxious which increases their chances of reacting to the next emotion-generating environmental trigger, which means more messes. Ugh. Years of that shit. No wonder everybody's walking around unhappy and narcissistic (next book). But not you. We're halting that process for you as we speak. And it's truly a knowledge-is-power situation, but the knowledge is useless if you don't practice. I mean it. You don't wanna be one of those grown-ass people that says shit like, "At least I know it's a problem." Ugh. I hate that. If you know it's a problem, why the hell aren't you doing something about it? Saying it isn't the same as choosing to behave in a new way. You see the problem? Change, muthafucker!

Okay, so the first step to understanding your emotions is simply naming them. Observe and describe your feelings in order to participate in your emotional experience in an effective way – tons of mindfulness skills, right? You already printed out or wrote out the emotion words you Googled, right? If you didn't – do it now. I'll wait.

Once you have your list of emotion words, I instruct people to read each of them and cross out the ones that are thoughts, not feelings. Every list sneaks in thoughts as feelings. It's an imperfect world. No biggie – remember from your "how" skills in the core mindfulness module: we practice "non-judgmentally," and a judgement is anything with an evaluative quality. Right/wrong, good/bad, worthwhile/worthless are all judgements anything that sounds like certainty, anything that sounds like "fact," anything that makes assumptions about another person's intentions. The usual suspects on lists are often in the fear words or anger words lists; like, "attacked" is often in anger words. But often, someone says they "feel attacked" when I'm challenging one of their long-standing beliefs – which is my job, they're paying me for it, and from my point of view, it's an act of love. How I go after that – and how I suggest you approach it – is by saying, "If you *think* I'm attacking you, how does that make you *feel?*" Then, they might get at the actual feeling and say, "defensive," "worried," "angry," etc. Now we got something I won't argue with them about because we validate all emotions. They're yours. It's not for me to define them.

There's a trend where people now say things like, "I don't feel heard," or "I don't feel seen," or "I don't feel safe," which is my pet peeve. Heard, seen, and safe are not feelings, dude. Just because I don't happen to agree with what you're saying doesn't mean I'm not listening. And just because I'm disagreeing with what you said, doesn't mean you're in danger, or "unsafe." By the way, the *world* isn't safe, and it's my job to help you learn the skills to deal with that reality and help you build a sense of freedom, confidence, and resilience. Working with me is not a conflict-free utopia where I think everything that comes outta your mouth is gold. But if you do find Unicorn Land, kindly let me know. Until then, my job is to create a tolerable amount of tension to the unhelpful beliefs you've carried around your whole life due to programming of our society. This friendly, loving tension and conflict is how change is achieved. You didn't come to me for help to stay the same, yo.

Other sneaky thoughts masquerading as feelings are words like, "invalidation" (see above pet peeves), "insult," "mean-spiritedness," to name a few. There are certain ones that I think of as "on the fence" between cognition and emotions, like, "indifference" (which might be better described as "apathy," but…), "depressed" (which is more of a diagnosis, than an emotion like "sad"), "anxiety" (which, if you were to say "scared," you'd probably feel it more), but if someone has established a new habit of mostly saying emotion words for feelings, I'll just let it go. At the end of the day, it's about separating thoughts from feelings and if they're mostly doing that, I'm not gonna interrupt them just to correct the odd outlier, y'know? Establishing healthy and productive ways of communicating, languaging, thinking, and managing emotions is what it's all about, not me being "right." I think "right" is bullshit anyway. You might disagree, and that's okay. See what I did there?

After building an emotional vocabulary and getting in the habit of reducing judgements and increasing using emotion words when we feel them, we use our core mindfulness skills and distress toler-ance skills to deal with painful emotions instead of choosing to add suffering to our pain. Here's how that works.

Remember that graph from the first lesson You're calm and cruising along at baseline, probably even in your wise mind, and then something happens where you get emotionally activated. Some people call this a "trigger." I've come to hate that reference because there's an assumption that the "trigger" is bad or at fault. What you get triggered by is about *your* history and programming, kid. Therefore, managing that trigger is *your* responsibility. That's why I like to language it "emotionally activated." Less of a responsibility-dump.

So something happens in your environment – let's stick with our earlier example where you are the pedestrian and the car runs the stop sign while you're crossing the street (by the way, I'm not even arguing that that person didn't make a mistake by running the stop sign; my point is so what? It's now your responsibility to behave in a way that keeps you out of harm's way and make sure this near miss doesn't tank your whole day of potential joy). So the car runs the stop sign and whizzes by you. Let's say you don't get hit, but you get activated emotionally, and now you are way off your baseline.

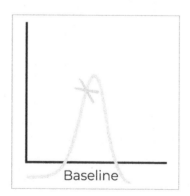

Baseline

What do you do next? An unskilled person might feel something, not name it, and yell or whip the driver the bird, possibly contributing to an altercation – which they chose to participate in. You, now equipped with some emotional intelligence skills, would stop, take a breath, and name your emotion (observe and describe). Just naming your emotion is an act of validating your emotional experience, and it will bring you closer to baseline.

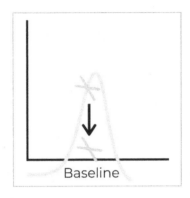

Baseline

It may or may not bring you all the way back to baseline, but chances are you won't be all the way calm yet. But the fact that you are just a little closer to your baseline means you are a bit less activated, and that ability to create even just a moment between the prompting event (car whizzing by you) and a behavioral reaction (whipping them the bird) means you have created a window of time where you could apply a skill to take you all the way back to calm.

I start people with three deep, abdominal breaths. Sound simple, right? Yes, it is simple – conceptually. But, in that moment, when your heart's beating faster and your fight or flight response has kicked in, we forget. We forget to breathe. We forget that we learned that three deep, abdominal breaths can have a positive impact on our central nervous system (CNS) and can disrupt that fight/flight response, preventing us from acting in a way that may not match our values and may not create the outcome we want. So breathe. The whole deal with DBT skills is we learn how to regulate our emotions when we have them, so we prevent mood-dependent decision-making. That's just a psych-way of saying when we act/react from a place of all emotionally jacked-up (mood-dependent), shit gets messy, and we often don't intend and don't like the outcome because we didn't decide from our wise mind (our set of values). And even if the person doesn't get outta the car and chase you down the street after you yelled and flipped them off, you'll probably have some shame about how you behaved if your actions didn't match the values you wrote down when you were calmly doing our first assignment about your values. Sure, you might justify it, "That asshole almost ran me over, so they deserved for me to..." yell, flip them off, throw a rock – whatever. But inside, you know that's not you. The shame has been banked. No one can make you do anything. You choose how you behave. We all do. End of story.

So, the most emotionally intelligent thing we can do is suspend all decision-making until we are back to baseline, or in our wise mind. Ya dig? You pickin' up what I'm puttin' down, Sparky? You can argue about right and wrong and deserves all day long, dude, believe me. I've done it – and my arguments are truly brilliant. But no one escapes themselves. We all gotta live with our truths. And most people's truth includes not acting from fear and behaving in an unloving way to another human being – hell, another living being, no matter what they "did." That's not just my opinion, dude. I think it's probably a universal truth. We can debate it if you want to sometime, 'cause I'd be interested in what you come up with.

So, it can help to think of your emotion(s) as a wave. It sweeps over you, but it's not who you are; it's something you are experiencing. You are separate from your emotion(s), and you are the boss. Emotions, even intense ones, often only last a matter of seconds, so ride it out. Don't push it down. Don't talk yourself out of it. Don't cling to it, either. Just notice it (observe) and name it (describe), and then breathe. Validation and then problem-solving. You do just that, and you're going to feel way more powerful and free.

Then, watch for your gremlin – that little voice that says shit like, "breathing doesn't work," "why were you afraid of that car; only wenises get scared," " you shoulda jacked that driver up!" Dumb programming shit like that. Those are just worry thoughts. And we know that thoughts aren't fact, they are just thoughts generated by feelings. There's no shame in thinking for just a moment that a car might hit you and it scares you, right? That doesn't make you weak; it makes you a human animal wired for survival. Just notice your gremlin (worry thoughts) and don't attach any meaning to them. They're not necessarily true. They don't have to mean anything – except that you had a fright. So what? You might even choose to feel grateful that you have a body that works well enough to automatically try to keep you out of danger. Fuck it. It's a moment. Move on with your day. That's radically accepting the world as it is instead of how you think it should be. That's you choosing to honor and regulate yourself and your emotional experience – regardless of what goes down in your environment. That's you powerful and free. Go you, Rockstar.

Okay, so I promised to teach you the pro-move of opposite action. Opposite action is a skill that's fascinating to teach because I always get a lot of resistance to it at first. Nearly 100 percent of the time, it's because on the first pass, folx misunderstand what it means. If I've already taught you that we validate every and all emotional experiences and feelings, you may think acting opposite to your feelings is a form of *in*validating those feelings. Nope. It's more complicated than that. And I already know you're smart and can keep up with complicated concepts, so hang with me on this for a sec.

Yes, a lot of the time the negative emotions we experience – fear, guilt, shame, sadness, and anger – are feelings we experience because we misunderstand/misinterpret an interaction with another human being. I know I get my feelings hurt a ton because of the way I anticipate or interpret how someone is talking to me or behaving toward me. They haven't always done something "wrong," per se, and I am hurt anyway. And sometimes they have crossed my boundary, said something I think is fucked up or rude, behaved in a way that doesn't match my values, or my gut is just like, "Uh-uh. Nope."

The same core mindfulness tools apply, though. I want to regulate my emotions, get back to my baseline/wise mind, before I decide how I want to act with that person. Even then, I have a choice. I do, however, want to make my decisions from that observer-stance, where I have just a little bit of distance from what I'm feeling so I can decide how I want to proceed and make sure my actions match my values. That way, my integrity and self-confidence are still protected, and I don't act in a way that causes me shame. Regardless of how the other person behaved, I want to be true to myself and not erode my self-esteem with shame. How do I do that? Well, one way I can disentangle myself from a situation someone else may have created is to employ my skill of opposite action. Even knowing I have that option to behave opposite of what I'm feeling empowers me – whether I use it or not.

The way opposite action works is I validate my negative emotion by observing it and describing it. Just name it, right? Then, if I so choose, I behave opposite to that emotion. So, if I'm afraid of something, I then go toward the thing that scares me. If I'm afraid to the point of the paralysis that often comes with overwhelm, I might break the scary thing up into bite-size pieces and just do the first little piece – just to start and break through the paralysis. What is so, so important is that I am not ignoring, pushing down, or talking myself out of the fear. I am naming the fear and choosing to do the scary thing anyway because one of my core values is courage – and I want to be brave. It goes without saying that I'm not talking about things that could kill me – nothing life-threatening, right? The thing is, we feel fear about so many things that aren't gonna kill us, so it's such a useful skill to learn how to employ our courage in those moments and do the scary thing anyway. Then we bank the self-confidence points in learning mastery in overcoming perceived obstacles to our goals and overall happiness and fulfillment in life. I don't get a lot of pushback in the fear-realm, because most people know we're automatically afraid, at first, of all the best, most exciting stuff in life. Most people know that if we never did anything we were afraid of, we'd never do any cool shit at all.

Where I start to get arguments is in the sadness camp. Sadness makes us kinda curl up into ourselves, right? We often wanna be left alone or just not do anything at all. I get that. I do. And we do want to validate and name that we feel sad. I think why people resist the idea of approaching sadness with something joyful is because there is so much anxiety from our loved ones when we are sad. Everybody's trying to cheer us up or remind us that life has joy and we "should" be grateful, blah blah blah. They unintentionally invalidate our sadness because it makes them nervous. And that sucks. If only everybody was emotionally intelligent enough to simply say, "That sucks. I'm sorry. Is there anything I can do for you?" and then just shut the fuck up and listen – or just sit with us and silently keep us company. Or hold us. Or make us a sandwich, whatever.

But prolonged and chronic sadness equals depression, and so many people have been depressed – like "diagnosibly" depressed – and we, as a society still, have almost no idea how to effectively deal with it. And now we just throw meds at depression right away. Mind you, medication does help depression. And if you've been depressed and meds helped you – I'm so glad to hear it. What I'm talking about is regular sadness – which is a natural emotion to experience from time to time. And when it's run of the mill sadness, it still hurts – no question. And if you're not depressed, you have the option of validating the sadness, disappointment, regret, or whatever and then choosing to problem-solve around it with a deliberate act of joy. That can be a powerful choice. And it can help it pass. You have to decide, from your wise mind values, when that's an option for you, kid. It's in your toolkit now.

You might not be surprised to learn that the most resistance I get when teaching opposite action is in the anger department. Shocker, right? Unlike sadness and fear, where the impulse is to hide and avoid, anger has a real activation to it. We get all fired up and wanna just give that person a piece of our mind, right? Or give that "jerk" a taste of their own medicine, etc. We wanna act, and we wanna act *now*. And if we act from that anger impulse, what often ends up happening? Messes. Shame. Regret. Embarrassment. Yuck. So, what opposite action gives us with our feelings of anger – even rage – is options and time. Remember, even intense emotions often have a shelf-life – a short one.

Often anger sticks around and we're lying awake at night thinking up all the things we "should" have said or wished we'd said because we didn't validate our anger and/or we haven't been taught the skills for how to effectively deal with it (more on that in the next module). So, even with opposite action, we validate that we're pissed. It's okay to be pissed, by the way. It doesn't make you an asshole, or even "an angry person." Anger is an emotion like any other emotion. In fact, since anger is the emotion that often alerts us that our boundaries are being crossed, I would argue that it's as important as fear in keeping us out of harm's way at times. We don't ignore any emotions, but for some reason, a lot of people are afraid of their anger.

Funny thing is, it's the stuffed anger that often results in blow-ups and shitty behavior you'll regret later. When you get skilled with validating your anger, you can calmly say things like, "What you're saying right now is pissing me off, so I'm gonna go cool off for ten minutes and come back to this." It's a powerful thing. Sometimes just saying, "Yeah, I don't agree with anything you're saying right now," stops a bully in their tracks. You'll learn that later. For now, your job is to observe and describe your anger – put words to it. Then, if you are trying out opposite action with anger, you might choose to stay away from the person pissing you off for a while. You might even choose to do something kind for someone – it doesn't have to be the person who pissed you off. You could be totally enraged by a family member and choose to make a card for a friend for their birthday or give your dog a good brushing and enjoy how happy it makes 'em. It's up to you. Again, it's important that you get that behaving opposite to your anger is not about being "polite" or "pleasing" to anybody else. It's fully about having the power of choice to disentangle yourself from an emotion that could negatively affect your whole day – if you let it. (Note: it's not necessarily opposite action, but I have found that writing out all the ugly thoughts, opinions, and beliefs that are generated by rage – and then tearing it up or safely burning – it has been quite relieving for many, many people, myself included. There's something about that exercise that is a physical representation of letting go of that anger because you get rid of the paper. Pen to paper seems to have more impact than typing it on yer phone or computer, but whatever. You choose.)

The last set of emotions we'll address with opposite action are guilt and shame. As I've probably said, these are tricky ones, mostly because they make our skin crawl like no other feelings, and we have a strong urge hide from that discomfort. Problem is, if we hide, we don't find and then we don't solve. We are all about the head-on problem-solving here, folx. Hello, have you met me? First, it's key that we figure out whether your emotions of guilt or shame are "justified" or "unjustified." This is completely defined by *you* and your wise mind values. It's not what I think, or your parents think, or anybody else thinks. If you behaved in a way that violated your values, then your guilt and/or shame is justified. If you value honesty and you lie to save your ass instead of admitting your mistake and eating your shit sandwich with some dignity, you're gonna feel shame unless you're a psychopath. I'm pretty sure you're not a psychopath. And I'm not talkin' about those white lies that spare someone's feelings like, "Wasn't that meme I sent you funny?" Sure. I thought it was kinda dumb, but whatever. I'm talking about the kind of lying that makes you feel a pit in your stomach and/or keeps you up at night. You wish you could go back and have a do-over – not 'cause yer obsessively anxious, but because you know, deep down, you fucked up. If that's the case, it's really easy. Go apologize. Go admit your mistake to the person. Go eat your humble pie with yer head held high because you did the courageous thing and also cleared your conscience. Well done. It was hard and you did it anyway. You repaired the mistake. Now, let it go and move on. Lesson learned.

Here's the other side of that – and this is the more opposite action-y piece with guilt and shame: If you did something that did not violate your values, yet you still feel guilty and ashamed. Now what? What does that even look like? Well, here's an example. Once when I was like fourteen, my friends and I were on a little road trip. We stopped at a gas station. I got a pack of gum and was holding it while my buddy paid for the gas. When we were back in the car, I realized I hadn't paid the quarter for the gum (yep, the gum was a quarter. It was on sale, but that's how old I am). I was mortified. I had "stolen" the gum. Fuck. I begged the driver to go back so I could pay for it but everybody in the car just laughed and I was almost in tears.

Is this a ridiculous story? Yes. Yes it is. Was the guilt and shame I felt real to me? Yes, indeed. That's why we validate all emotions. They are felt by the feeler, so no one can say what's real except the person feeling the feels. But here's the kicker: Did I violate my wise mind values? What do you think? Certainly stealing violates my values unless I'm starving or something and steal a loaf of bread. But it was a mistake. It was an accident. I didn't do it on purpose, and I would have preferred to go back and repair that transgression – but to beat myself up the way I did was unnecessary. I would now argue that it was even ego, meaning that I had such a view of myself as "someone who would never steal," so morally virtuous, that I "deserved" punishment for a mistake. Puke. Just chew the gum and get over yourself, angsty teen J.J.

Where this story falls short for this example is that the task to get over "unjustified" guilt and shame – that is, when you do *not* violate your values – is to do the thing that causes the unjustified guilt and shame over and over and over until you build up your tolerance to unjustified guilt and shame. Funny, huh? In this case, it wouldn't be wise to steal gum everywhere I go to get used to it, but it would be wise to not beat myself up for a mistake. Make mistakes, own 'em, let 'em go, and move on. You get it? Where do you find unjustified feelings of guilt and shame in your life? Getting a "B?" Pronouncing someone's name wrong? Singing offkey? If you didn't violate your values, then do that thing more 'til that skin-crawling feeling goes away or at least lessens. That's opposite action.

There. Now you have a toolbox full of emotion regulation skills too. When you put 'em all together and put 'em into action, they look like this:

What Happened – Describe the facts of the event that got you emotionally dysregulated/activated/triggered. Do it without judgements/evaluations/opinions/beliefs.

Name the Emotions – What did you feel? Make sure they're emotion words and not thoughts.

Interpretations – Now list your opinions, beliefs, assumptions, and judgements. It's okay if they're petty, just know they're thoughts, not facts.

Body Activation – What do you feel in your body? Where? Do you recognize that sensation as going with a certain emotion(s)? What's your face doing? Posture? Gestures?

Impulses – What do you wish you could do? It's okay if it's dark, it's just an urge – hopefully you don't choose to do it.

Choice of Behavior – What did you do? And if you gave in to your impulse/urge, say so – and how *that* made you feel. If you wisely chose an action that matched your values despite your dark urges, then celebrate that and name those emotions.

Impact – How'd you feel after? Body, mind, emotions? Are you wiped out? Energized? Confused?

Homework: Now pick times in real life and recently when you got emotionally activated and write out everything above. It doesn't have to take long, just be as specific as you can. The sooner you do it following the event, the more useful this gets. Do a bunch of 'em. All the young folx I work with do this exercise constantly. It becomes habit quickly, and it's one of the most useful tools in the kit. Good luck.

Now that we have the core mindfulness skills, the distress tolerance skills, and the emotion regulation skills, it's time to add the wild card: another person. We now enter into the final module: Interpersonal Effectiveness Skills.

9

A – ACTIVATION OF SELF

It's time to put everything you've learned into practice as we add the element of another person to our skillset, and you're gonna need it, 'cause other people bring all *their* stuff to the mix.

First, go back and review your core mindfulness skills. Can you do it by yourself yet? Wise mind, first. Then, what do we do? And how do we do it? If you can't name 'em yet, go back to the beginning of Chapters 4, 5, 6, 7, or 8 by yourself 'cause there's no way I'm givin' you the answer here again. Do the damn work.

Now then, why do we want to learn the Interpersonal Effectiveness Skills module? Because all we do all day long is interact with other humans. Don't you think it might be useful to learn how to do it skillfully? I know I'm preaching to the choir on this one, 'cause here you are on Chapter 9 of this book – obviously you're motivated. Kudos, by the way. My frustration is that most people (again, not someone rad like you) still do not see the basic value in developing skills to communicate effectively with their other human counterparts. Most people are just posers walking around like they know what they're doing and they're doing it well. And not just young people. For young folx, it's kind of acceptable to not know what's up because yer just trying to figure it out, right? Problem is that adults taught you to hide the fact that you don't know what's going on and aren't supposed to because the twenties are super hard – especially the first half. They kinda mellow out a bit after that. Jesus, I think life before twenty-five – all of it – was just a constant struggle. Don't listen to media on this young-worship thing, dude, I'm telling you. Aging can be so enriching and exciting and powerful – if you choose to listen to yer gut (wise mind) and employ your courage (notice, name, and emotionally regulate your fear. Again, yer welcome).

The other part of life that can rock is kick ass relationships. Family relationships can be so supportive and rewarding and reliable, but if your family blows, you can always choose a new one as a young adult or adult. Queer culture has been doing that forever, and we all owe the pioneers a hat tip, my friends. Quality of relationships can translate directly to a higher quality of life. Your hard times are easier to ride out when you know someone's got yer back, and the joyful times can be ten times more fun, silly, and full of love and laughter with the right people close to you. Close friends can hold us up when we're scared and sad, they can cheer us on when we're brave and achieve, and if they're a quality friend, they'll call us out when we have our head up our ass. The best friends have the courage to challenge us when we're fucking up. Do you agree with that? I think it lacks courage to sit by and watch someone you love self-destruct. Who cares if they get mad? Who cares if they yell at you? Who cares if you were wrong and they're doin' okay? Yer not gonna die. The worst that can happen is the friendship ends, and if it does over somethin' like that, you seriously dodged a bullet on that one. Their fragility woulda come out some other way sooner or later.

So what's this skillset all about? Thrilled you asked. The overarching point to developing skills for interpersonal effectiveness is two sets of three. We wanna learn skills to:

1. Ask for things we want.
2. Say no.
3. Resolve conflict.

And the goal is to:

1. Meet our objectives above, while

2. Keeping a positive relationship, and

3. Maintaining our self-respect.

Much like all of this emotional intelligence training, these are easy concepts to grasp while reading them and tougher to implement in the moment of high emotion. This, and most things, get easier with practice. Let's get into it, because this stuff is so useful – like every day and with all people useful. No shit.

So have you ever been in an interaction with someone else, your emotions start to get activated, shit starts to go south, and now you're in a full on fight/argument with that person? And you know it's not going well – you can totally feel that, and you honestly have no idea how it got that bad that fast? Hell yeah, you have. We all have. Sometimes we didn't have any clue at all that it was even gonna be a conflict and now it's gone straight to hell in a handbasket. Ugh. It truly sucks when interactions go down like that. The worst part is, not only did we not intend for it to be a yelling match, we have no idea what to correct to try to make it go better the next time. That can create hurt and sadness and a perceived helplessness that makes us pretty damn resistant to trying *that* again. Nothing gets resolved, and both people walk away with crummy feels – maybe even walking on eggshells around that person for a while – both of you knowing there's that *thing* between you. Yuck.

Let me tell you the #1 reason those kinds of ruptures happen. Neither of you had a defined objective going into that interaction. Now I'm not talkin' to that other person; I'm talkin' to you. I'm telling you that it is totally your responsibility – before you ask someone for something, say "no" to someone about something, or want to resolve a conflict with someone – to get into your wise mind, knowing what your values are, and define your objective for that conversation. Figure out if it's an ask, a say no, or a conflict resolution talk. This, in and of itself, will set the tone for a grounded calm you going in.

You also want to define what's most important to you: your objective getting met, maintaining the relationship, or maintaining your self-respect. Take a minute to rank those in order of importance. But even if relationship or self-respect are number one, you always want to go in knowing what your objective IS – what do you want the outcome to be? You might not get it, but you want to know what it is. You won't get it if you don't know what it even *is* going in. I cannot stress the importance of this enough.

So, this is what to do before you get face-to-face with the person:

1. Define your objective. What specific result

or change do you want from this interaction? Are you asking for something? Are you saying no to something? Are you wanting to resolve a conflict?

2. Impact on the relationship. How do you want this person to feel about you after the interaction is done? Do you want to keep the relationship in positive standing? What will you have to do to keep it in positive standing? Does this match your values?

3. Liking yourself. How do you want to behave that supports your self-respect and your values? What will work/is effective? How do you want to feel about yourself when this is all over?

Just asking yourself these questions will get you clear on how you want to present yourself and your objective(s). You may feel nervous about the interaction, and that's okay. That's natural. We all feel nervous about the possibility of confronting someone or behaving vulnerably. I've been teaching this shit for hella years and am an expert communicator, and sometimes I still get nervous too. The thing is, though, I've practiced this thousands of times, so I've seen how well it works and how much it improves my most valued relationships, so I have my own experiential data I've collected. Once I admit to myself that I'm nervous (observe and describe) and breathe to calm down (regulate my emotion to bring myself closer to my baseline/wise mind), I am ready to most effectively participate in the conversation. I am present, I am remembering and trusting how many times these skills have worked, and I can be brave – even still feeling some nerves.

You don't have *your* experiences and data about these skills yet – I get that. And I don't expect you to just take my word for it. All I need from you is to suspend your "certainty" that you've already tried this a million times with this person and it "never works." Maybe it never worked – yet. Maybe it never worked yet because you didn't have these skills under yer belt. Maybe. Maybe is the window of hope cracked open just the tiniest bit to allow for the possibility that with new tools in your toolbox, change *can* happen. That's all I need from you – the willingness to try it. Scratch that – I generally think "try" is horseshit. "Try" is something people say *instead* of doing. I want you to do the skills. Do your best. Dude, what's the worst that can happen? It goes the same way it did before and nothing changes? Big whoop. That's the same place you are now. You got nothin' to lose, yo.

Okay, so there's another set of ideas we want you to analyze before you go into your interaction with the person: shit that can get in the way of you maximizing your effectiveness. There are a handful of things that could tank your win, so let's go over 'em.

STUFF THAT JAMS US UP

No skill

This doesn't mean you're not motivated for the conversation to go well, it just means that before this, you were not taught the skills so you probably didn't stand much of a chance of getting your objectives met. Not your fault. Not for lack of wanting. You just didn't have a full toolbox like you do now (or will after this chapter).

Your Gremlin (Rick Carson's book: **Taming Your Gremlin.** *Read it) – worry thoughts are a mutherfucker.*

You gotta remember that you're probably going to be nervous and that fear generates worry thoughts. That doesn't make 'em true. We validate the fear and just notice that the fear is making hella weird, dark shit whiz through our brains. Just observe that. Breathe. Let 'em go. You don't know what the other person's thinking/feeling, you can't predict the future, and you're not stupid. Don't let your gremlin trick you into believing that you can't

do scary things. You can. And you won't die...
probably.

Feelings

If you do not regulate your fear, anger, or any
other emotions skillfully, they will push you off baseline (out of your wise mind) and there you'll float,
sayin' shit you don't mean, regretting attempting
this, pissed at me, mired in shame. Go through the
emotional balance exercise in the last chapter to get
your feelings in check before you are with the person
– you will not be sorry you did.

Flip-flopping

This one's basically the result emotions not being
in check. Fear is usually how we get onto the tread-
mill to nowhere of indecision. You already decided to
do this, you're just scared. Breathe and go back to
basics. Do the emotional balance exercise and then
define your objective of this conversation.

Wild Card

The other person brings their shit into this
conversation, so sometimes even when you deliver
your objectives super skillfully, they might not work
because we can't control other people. You might be

in a lower power position: like with your parents, or a teacher, or a boss. Sometimes they have the final say no matter what. Sucks, and it's true (radical acceptance). A friend might not like you or talk shit about you if they give you what you want (not a particularly decent friend, though, if that happens). You might need to negotiate or compromise a bit (more on that later).

Like I said, these factors can get in the way of you behaving effectively, but going through them ahead of time can set you up to conquer 'em all. Knowledge is power, folx.

Before we get into the full-on meat and potatoes of these skills to activate yourself (any Midwesterners here? Californians don't say meat and potatoes like that.), you might consider practicing some of these in low/no consequence environments – that means strangers. And if just reading that flips yer shit, you want to do it before you hit the "stage." I'm talking simple shit, too. Just open your mouth when you disagree with someone, or ask someone for help, or politely ask your sibling to stop doing that thing that's annoying you (don't call them "annoying," since we're practicing a non-judgmental stance, right?). One of the one's Linehan lists is "While talking with someone, change the subject." I love that one, because I always evaluated that as "rude," so I never did it. Now I do it whenever I want – no nervousness, no shame. These are easy-peasy, lemon-squeezy. And if you disagree, I suggest you do a ton of 'em before you go ask your dad for money, or ask your friend to stop asking you about a romantic relationship that ended, or a teacher/professor asks you why you didn't turn in your paper – you feel me?

The heart and soul of interpersonal effectiveness skills is an assertiveness formula with the acronym D.E.A.R. It's not mine; it's Linehan's – and someday I'll make up a hip-er one for it, but not today. So, what does D.E.A.R. stand for? Well, my friend, I'm so pleased you asked.

D: DESCRIBE

This is the same "describe" as the one from the core mindfulness skills: observe and describe. You are describing the situation. You tell the other person what's up on your end. Remember: just the facts, not judgements.

E: EXPRESS

We're still judgement-free here, but you do want to express your feelings and opinions. And remember, the way to express an opinion effectively is to say "I think" before your opinion. Don't try to pass it off as fact or a feeling. You're allowed to not like something the person did, you just say, "I didn't like" this thing they did, not "You were mean to..." Ya dig? We want to express ourselves with "I want," not "I need you to" or the bane of my existence: "You need to." (No *I* don't need that, Karen. *You* might want me to, and that's not going to happen.) Also, for the purposes of practice, we leave out "shoulds" and "can't," because one's an opinion (that shames) and the other addresses "ableness" and usually isn't true.

A: ASSERT

This is the part where you do the actual asking for what you want or the saying no directly. The big thing to remember here is that other people can't read your mind, nor is it their responsibility to guess. It is your responsibility to communicate your wants and don't wants clearly and specifically – even when you're scared. It might be difficult at first, and you may have an urge to get resentful that you "even have to ask." Too bad. Notice the urge, regulate the emotions, and ask/say no anyway. This maximizes your chances of getting taken seriously as a mature and emotionally intelligent person with integrity. Suck it up, Buttercup. It gets much easier with practice – *and* you'll feel proud of yourself when you do this regardless of outcome.

R: REINFORCE

Basic psych says we reinforce the behaviors we want to continue, and we mostly ignore the behaviors we don't want to continue. This riffs on that by rewarding the person beforehand. A basic "reinforce" thanks the person for giving you what you want before they've given you what you want. "I'd appreciate it" or just "Thank you" is a simple reinforce, which we'll get into in a bit.

Another way to reinforce is to describe the positive or negative consequences or effects of you getting what you want or not getting what you want. I know, at first, this might sound like it's kinda threatening, but there are ways to do it where it isn't. You just wanna grease the wheels for the person feeling happy ahead of time for accepting what you want and giving it to you.

So what does one of these look/sound like in real life? Let's try one. Let's say your parent comes into your room without asking or knocking no matter how many times you've asked or demanded they don't do that. Well, before we confront them what are your steps?

What is your objective? Simple. Instead of just walking into your room, you want them to knock and wait until you say, "Come in," right? If you just ask for the knock alone, they might do it and just rush in without your permission, and that's damn near the thing that's happening now, right? You see how we want to get as specific as possible with our objective? Think it all the way through while you're alone.

In regard to the relationship and your self-respect, you may think neither matter. I can make a case that even if you say you don't care that you currently scream "Get out. You never knock! This is my room!" it can't be great for your relationship with that parent to start any interaction yelling. Immediate heated conflict. And though it's easy to validate your frustration with that abrupt invasion of your space, it is their house. More importantly, you sound like a child. As you're growing up, you are learning to conduct yourself in a more mature way – not for anyone other than yourself, really. You wouldn't scream at a friend for doing that; you'd look like a jackass. Also, adults dismiss young people who scream, yell, and whine. Let's see if you can improve your chances of being treated like more of an adult by conducting yourself like one.

Now, is it an "ask" or a "say no?" I think you could make an argument for either, and it's your choice. For the purposes of this exercise, I think it's easiest to treat it as a firm "ask." Yeah? You good with that?

Lastly, in pre-interaction prep, we want to address those factors that might get in your way of being effective in this case. Of the five listed a few pages back, I see two glaring possible obstacles. Go back and review the Stuff That Jams Us Up list and see which ones I mean.

Yep – three and five: Feelings and Wild Card. You're already super pissed they keep coming in your room. You're frustrated because you've asked a bunch of times already, so you might feel helpless too. What other feelings from your list apply here? Go check and pick a couple more. The parent(s) piece is the wild card because you can't control them, and you, my dear, are on the lower end of a power dynamic because they are the parents and they are in charge. This may not work – *even* if you deliver your D.E.A.R. "perfectly."

This brings me to an important point to keep in mind, and I tell everyone this: you basically have *two* opportunities for a "win" in this interaction. First, deliver your D.E.A.R. in the most skillful way you can that matches your wise mind values, and collect the self-confidence points for courage 'cause facing fear of conflict is brave. Second, you get the outcome you want. One is infinitely more important than two. Wait, what? Yes. We can't control other people, and we don't want to cling to an outcome. We can want an outcome without being super-attached to it. That's wise mind, remember? We are at peace with the outcome. We might not like it, but we accept it. Acceptance is not approval. It's just calm with what is. You can even kinda loathe it and still be at peace with it. That's mindfulness. People always say, "just let it go," without teaching us how. This is how. Wrap yer head around that. Win number one is more important than any outcome. You did your best and can be proud – even when things don't go your way. This is a life lesson about freedom, kiddo. True freedom.

Okay, so let's go.

D: Describe – just the facts of the situation.

"You continue to come into my room, even though I've asked you to knock first."

E: Express – feelings and opinions

"I don't like that." Or "That makes me so mad."

A: Assert – the actual "ask"

"Please knock and then wait to come in until I say so."

R: Reinforce – thank 'em beforehand or describe consequences (positive or negative)

"I'd appreciate it." Or, "I think things will go smoother between us when you do." Or, "There's just this constant tension between us every time you don't."

Ya dig? The real beauty of this is that most parents, when addressed in this way, will agree to the knock and come in plan, and then forget and do it again the next day – no one's perfect. Not to worry. Then your D.E.A.R. looks/sounds like this:

D – "You've made the commitment to me to knock and wait' til I say 'Okay' before coming in my room, yet you are not sticking to your commitment."

E- "I feel bummed and frustrated because I believed you when you said you would."

A – "Will you please do what you said you were going to do by knocking and waiting for my okay to come in here?"

R – "I know I'll appreciate that, and I'll remember to thank you when you do it."

Right? Now, of course, you will use your words – and if we were doin' this in-person, I'd help you construct your D.E.A.R. in a way that's authentic to you. For now, try repeating the words written here. Even try it in the mirror. If you feel awkward, you're doing it correctly. It's new, so reduce your awkwardness by repeating it lots of times. Then use this structure to make one in your words. Then the mirror-thing again to get used to it.

This same structure can be used for anything with anyone. And it totally works. I shit you not, you'll be shocked the first time you pull it off. Good luck. I'm so excited for you. Shoot me a text and tell me how it went – 510-595-7594, or email at drjjkelly.com. I love hearing wins with this shit. So empowering.

Now there are more details that Linehan includes.

- Don't lie or exaggerate

- Don't over apologize
- Appear confident
- Negotiate when yer outta options
- Don't judge
- Do a tone check
- Ignore their attempts to divert

Yes to all these. And they are easy and quick to teach in person, but there's one I do want to explain here: broken record.

Broken record is a skill for when you've already delivered your D.E.A.R. and now the other person starts "dancing." You just said your ask or say no, and now they begin to talk – and it's usually pretty defensive. People's behaviors range on a spectrum, like most things, but most folx will feel a little anxious when confronted. You, with your new skillset, will probably see it. They probably will not. They might do any number of things like, start explaining or justifying their behaviors you just addressed. They might bring up some past shitty behavior *you* engaged in (attack/divert) once. They might say they'll do your thing if you do *their* thing. Most of their behaviors will be slightly to grossly off-point. Do not take that hook.

If they're speedily talking, just let them run it out a little. Say nothing. Don't justify anything they're saying by responding. When you do see a natural opening, calmly take it. And here's what you do. You repeat your D.E.A.R. verbatim. Yup, I'm deadass. Word for frickin' word; repeat your exact D.E.A.R. again. Now see what happens. What people always ask when learning "broken record" is, "If you just keep saying the same thing like a robot, isn't that gonna piss the other person off?" You'd think so, wouldn't you? Funny thing is, if a person's "dancing" like that, they're anxious. And almost without fail, they will not even notice repetition. I know. Crazy, right? But I'm telling you they won't. Now, when you've practiced doin' D.E.A.R.s for a bit, you will notice how sometimes you will naturally not need to say every D and E, and you can just jump right to the Assert. Practice the whole thing first, but you'll see how that happens. And when you're comfortable with that, you're gonna naturally do your broken records that way: right to the Assert without the Describe and Express. And that'll work great. Even punchier. I'm a huge fan of "potent and concise," so I'm always looking for the fewest words possible to make all my points. I think it's more impactful and useful; that's just me. You do you. And now you'll do you even better. Hell yeah. Go you. You really cannot believe how skilled a person can get at this. The "docs" at UnorthoDocs (former psychotherapy "patients") do these on our coaching calls – and because they're group calls, everyone benefits. They've gotten so proficient, they pee-coach each other. It's truly amazing! They also write 'em out on our private Facebook group – which is hella brave and also benefits the speaker and the whole group. Just when you think you've mastered the D.E.A.R., you break through to a whole new level of skill and authenticity. Thank you, Marsha.

Your homework assignment here is simple: do hella D.E.A.R.s! Plan 'em out. Write 'em down. Deliver them. Assess what worked and what didn't. Tweak it and do another one and another one. Welcome to the rest of your life.

We're gonna ride that celebration wave in Chapter 10, where we take the more powerful, skillful you to superpower territory.

10

L – LIKE YOURSELF AND LEAD

You have already exponentially increased your emotional intelligence. What you've read in previous chapters has taught you how to increase your awareness and notice when you are truly present in your life. You have learned to separate feelings from thoughts and thoughts from fact. Yes, you came to me "gifted." It's why you picked up this book. The thing is that "gifted," in our society, usually refers to intellect – IQ. Sure, sometimes it can refer to musicianship, or artistic talent, or dance or other sports. Mostly, though, it means smart. What special people like you and I and the young people I work with know, though, is that you can't think your way outta all life's problems. Sometimes you don't follow all the rules. And a lot of times, you get in trouble when you don't. And a lot of times you don't fit it. People who do follow rules think yer weird. And what I teach gets you to a place where you can say...Fuck 'em. And you are genuinely free from caring what others think.

What I teach is emotional intelligence. Yes, I taught you mindfulness, how to language a non-judgmental stance, and how to name your feelings and manage them – even when they're strong. Then I taught you the formula for asking for what you want and saying no – in a new, more effective way. And as you practice these skills and rack up the wins with your brave risk-taking and experience, you will get stronger and stronger.

Yeah, but stronger in what? Stronger for what? What do you think the definition of emotional intelligence is? Understanding and managing your emotions – yes. Why? You're already smart and can probably achieve your academic and career goals just by being "gifted." So, what is the practical value of emotional intelligence? People in huge companies out here in California talk emotional intelligence – or EQ – all the time. They work at Google and Facebook, and Salesforce and Oracle. I've met and worked with a bunch of 'em. They say "EQ" a lot. I haven't found them to be particularly emotionally intelligent, though. Most seemed pretty lost to me – and not happy. But what is happiness? Is happiness meeting goals or getting the sweet job and career, marrying the smart, beautiful person, taking adventure holidays?

I've taught you these skills because they help you pay attention and shift your perspective. These skills teach you knowledge and mastery with your emotional experiences to unlearn society's programming and choose what you value. Then you can mindfully decide what behaviors match those values and how to stick up for yourself when you're met with someone whose values may not match yours. I believe this frees you up to start digging and exploring who you are and who you want to become. Has anyone ever asked you who you think you are? Did they stick around to listen to the answer? Did they listen and seem genuinely interested in what you had to say? I'm hoping those are all "yes." If not, it doesn't matter because you need time to find out who you are in order to authentically answer that anyway.

In our society, we spend so much time trying to avoid our feelings because we don't have the first clue what to do with 'em. No one teaches us that. Well, now you know a *lot*. And when you practice these skills in this book in a disciplined way that becomes habit over time, your sense of self-esteem, self-respect, and self-confidence will naturally become fortified, and you will notice, in yourself, a greater capacity to experience joy. Think about that a sec: you learned the skills to like yourself – isn't that the basis for increasing one's capacity for experiencing joy? I strongly believe it is.

Most people are wandering around this earth scared, striving, and unhappy. They appear to have it all, so why the hell are they unhappy? I believe it's because they are so focused on the external validation of achievement of "success" – as defined by society – that they are disconnected from themselves and what brings them joy. They may have it "all," but they don't enjoy it. How sad. And that's *most* people. And that will *not* be you. You now know how to tap into your connection with yourself – and it's through your emotions. Our emotions guide us to what brings us joy and they signal to us when we don't feel it, too. Pretty useful stuff. To use the signaling of our emotions, we first must get at why we avoid them instead of acknowledging, validating, and effectively manage them. These skills are not designed to help you not feel emotions. This is not to prevent you feeling anything. These skills help you to welcome in feeling everything. You can feel each emotion, all emotions, all the way. You can enhance your life, each day, by feeling all the feels. You don't have to act on every single one – particularly if the impulse does not match your values. But we all have light and dark inside us, and you don't have to run away from the negative feelings now that you know how to manage them. Do you get how incredible that is?

And once you start getting good at these skills, you're gonna see something incredible happen.

People will be curious about you and drawn to you – wondering what you have that they don't. Because the false belief in society is that only some people have that allure. Not true. We all have the capacity to have that sparkle, that specialness, that magnetism, that shine, that light. When you have a healthy regard and respect for yourself and behave according to what you truly believe in, you radiate joy.

Haven't you already noticed a difference in yourself from when you were on page one of this book and now? When I teach my eight-week course of this, people start to notice the change in week two or three. Even the people who know the people taking the course notice. They notice and they say something. It's nuts. That's why I keep doin' it. Best job ever.

So, when you start to change and grow and expand and laugh a little easier and act a little kinder – people notice and want to be around you. And you want to be around them. Yer not all awkward and self-conscious anymore. You're confident – probably goofy. And you don't give a fuck if people talk shit about you because you are solid in who you are. You have learned to look for your validation inside of you, instead of being dependent on external validation, which erodes self-esteem and takes us out of our true selves.

When you like yourself – like, for *real* – you will feel full to the brim with joy. You'll wanna play and laugh – kinda like young kids play. It's awesome. And when your cup is full, it starts to overflow. And *that* is when you will experience a natural desire to give. Generosity is the natural byproduct of joy and liking yourself. Some people perform generous acts because they think it makes them a "good person," and to some extent, I think that's true. Might be better to have a world where people are so interested in other people thinking they're a "good person" that they perform generous acts all over town. Probably better than everybody just running around being dicks to each other and not caring. But I think the best world is one where we are taught the tools to like ourselves, and then we can discover who we are, what our unique talents are, and then generously share them with all other humans – all living things – all things. I believe our purpose, your purpose, my purpose, is to:

1. Learn the tools to like yourself and increase your ability and capacity for joy
2. Explore your authentic self to discover what your unique talents are so you can develop them and master them to
3. Share them with the world
4. Heal the world

What else could it be? I mean it. Why the hell are

we here other than to find our superpower and share it in service to all humanity?

Here's a secret, too. When you experience that natural urge to give that bubbles up when you truly like yourself, it heals you too. The catch is, though, you can't engage in a pure act of giving *for* the purpose of receiving. The only way to receive from giving is to give with no expectation of receiving. Now, don't freak out and think what I'm saying is have no boundaries and just be a doormat and martyr yourself for everybody else. That bullshit is about you – and it's ego and super narc-y and gross.

True giving is about them. True giving comes from a happy person, and happy people like themselves and give to everyone around them – including themselves. It's when your internal gas tank is so full, the overflow is the natural thing you give. It's not when yer gas tank is on "E" with the red light on and you burn out sacrificing yourself "for" others. That ain't for others, friend. That's all you. And yuck. That does no one no good, you hear me? Don't be a gross, withered, unhappy drone of an adult. Be a growing, changing, brave, and juicy adult who laughs all the time. Feel the joy that comes from liking yourself. And then feel the joy that comes from sharing yourself and your superpowers with others. You can lead by your example. None of the shit that bothers you now will bother you anymore. Work the skills. Work the shit outta them.

11

NOW WHAT?

O kay, yer either pumped or puked due to that last paragraph. If you thought, "Barf," I expect you'll read no further. I respect that. We may not be each other's people. If you agreed, were inspired, or thought, "Well, maybe..." Here we are. You've read the book and have probably tried some of the skills, and I'm hoping you rocked some. It's not easy on yer own, so... nice. If you don't continue practicing the skills, you probably can guess what's gonna happen. Nothing. At least I hope it's just nothing and not you going around in your life thinkin' that everybody else has it figured out, and you're the fucked up one. My guess is you've had enough of that.

The people I work with, we embrace the term "misfit" because we've all been judged as weirdos –

even though we're "gifted." I always use air-quotes because I think we're all perfectly imperfect. Society thinks we're freaks because *society* is hella fucked up. Everybody's in a race to the hell of making themselves exactly the same as everybody else instead of embracing our badass one-of-a-kind beautiful snowflake perfection. Mother Nature doesn't fuck up, yo. She's perfect. So is God, Source, The Universe, or whomever you believe created us. You are not a mistake. You are you, so you are perfect.

Get yer shit together and start learning and liking who you are, dammit. You already learned so much in this book – just practice the skills. And if yer having trouble doing that, text or email me and I'll see what I can do to help. Or find someone near you who's real and teaches DBT. Or go learn to meditate. Do something different. If the same means you're suffering, do something different – we like different. And keep in mind that you learned not to like yourself from years of practice and programming. It's gonna take a minute to undo that. Be patient with yourself and compassionate with your mistakes. And please, please celebrate your wins. Make up a dance that you do whenever you nail it – anything in the plus column gets a dance or whatever method you choose to mark celebration. I'm a big fan of suggesting people go get themselves a cake and have them write, "Congratulations, [your name]. You Rock." Take it home for yourself or to share with others. Is that cheesy? You bet yer ass, it is! This world could do with a *lot* more cheese (says the Wisconsin-born doc). I love anything that's goofball-driven; the wackier the better. But, cake is not necessary. You do you. Just do something.

12

BLOWIN' OUT CANDLES

O h, kiddo, here we are. We've been through so much. Hopefully we'll meet again. Next week's my birthday, and here's what I wish. I'll tell you now. I know I'm not supposed to tell anyone my wish or it won't come true, but I've always thought that's horseshit and I'm punk as fuck, anyway.

My wish for you is that you use what you've learned about self-discovery here – and anywhere – and practice, apply, and do. When you act – even when you're afraid – you can transform yourself into a healthy human that's full of life and joy. You can genuinely love and like yourself. Don't listen to people that say shit like, "No one likes themselves..." I've heard tons of people try to sell that shit to me. I've had doctors who charge money to help people be happy laugh in my face – seriously.

But, I like myself. And it's not because tons of fucked up shit hasn't happened to me. It has. Happiness is a choice. Think of all the negative messages coming to us from society and the media – all that programming. It's easy to get depressed – and hard to get out. Anybody can hate themselves; it's not an accomplishment. It's probably our default. Fight for yourself. Fight until it's habit and the momentum is going in the like-yourself-direction. Then bask in your glory and keep practicing the skills because we're never done. It's something we do, but we're not done until we're *done*, you feel me? And even then, I'm not even sure we're done. I dunno.

So go experience joy and let your happiness become contagious and your enthusiasm for who you are – flaws and all – will draw people to you that want to learn your secret. And you have no need, whatsoever, to keep it a secret. Keep increasing your awareness of yourself, your values, your emotional experiences, and how they guide you, and *choose* how you want to behave in your life. Weather pain that comes up with dignity, grace, and even humor until it passes, and you learn from it. When yer a pro, you'll be in the thick of the pain and ask yourself, "What am I supposed to learn from this?" Learn to identify and accept *all* of your emotional experiences and manage them deftly in order to reduce the shame reactivity and increase your self-confidence and joy. Know and practice the art of healthy confrontation and conflict to make the most out of your relationships with friends, family, teachers, bosses, strangers – everybody. And lead the world around you into an era of happiness and joy just by liking and being yourself – no matter what anyone else says. Get real. Do real. Be real.

ACKNOWLEDGMENTS

Thanks to The Author Incubator team. Angela Lauria, thank you for your friendship and inspiration to evoke change. Cory Hott, my editor and friend, thank you for your patience and hard work. I appreciate you.

I wanna thank my brother, Sam, too. Laughing with you is one of my greatest pleasures in life. Your sweetness gives me hope for the equality of the future.

Thank you to our friend Nathan Prebonick for the image of his painting on this book, and the painting in my room. You've tapped into source with your work – it's sublime.

ABOUT THE AUTHOR

Dr. J.J. Kelly is a licensed clinical psychologist and emotional intelligence skills training expert. Dr. Kelly is the CEO & Founder of UnorthoDocs, Inc., a punk alternative to traditional psychotherapy and mental health practices. UnorthoDocs, Inc. focuses on group processes, mentorship, peer-coaching, community outreach, laughter & love. J.J. is a proud resident of Oakland, California.

ABOUT DIFFERENCE PRESS

Difference Press is the exclusive publishing arm of The Author Incubator, an educational company for entrepreneurs – including life coaches, healers, consultants, and community leaders – looking for a comprehensive solution to get their books written, published, and promoted. Its founder, Dr. Angela Lauria, has been bringing to life the literary ventures of hundreds of authors-in-transformation since 1994.

A boutique-style self-publishing service for clients of The Author Incubator, Difference Press boasts a fair and easy-to-understand profit structure, low-priced author copies, and author-friendly contract terms. Most importantly, all of our #incubatedauthors maintain ownership of their copyright at all times.

LET'S START A MOVEMENT WITH YOUR MESSAGE

In a market where hundreds of thousands of books are published every year and are never heard from again, The Author Incubator is different. Not only do all Difference Press books reach Amazon bestseller status, but all of our authors are actively changing lives and making a difference.

Since launching in 2013, we've served over 500 authors who came to us with an idea for a book and were able to write it and get it self-published in less than 6 months. In addition, more than 100 of those books were picked up by traditional publishers and are now available in bookstores. We do this by selecting the highest quality and highest potential applicants for our future programs.

Our program doesn't only teach you how to write a book – our team of coaches, developmental editors, copy editors, art directors, and marketing experts incubate you from having a book idea to being a published, bestselling author, ensuring that the book you create can actually make a difference in the world. Then we give you the training you need to use your book to make the difference in the world, or to create a business out of serving your readers.

ARE YOU READY TO MAKE A DIFFERENCE?

You've seen other people make a difference with a book. Now it's your turn. If you are ready to stop watching and start taking massive action, go to http://theauthorincubator.com/apply/.

"Yes, I'm ready!"

OTHER BOOKS BY DIFFERENCE PRESS

The Successful Canna-preneur: The Practical Guide to Thrive in the Legal Cannabis Space by JM Balbuena

Healing the Healer Within: 8 Steps to Unleash Your Potential by Dr. Cheri McDonald

Ocean of Possibilities: Maximize Natural Cancer Healing with Marine Organisms and Functional Medicine by Heather Moretzsohn

Will I Ever Get Pregnant?: The Smart Woman's Guide to Get Pregnant Naturally Over 40 by Tsao-Lin E. Moy

The Evolving Home: The Conscious Design Guide to Restoring Function and Comfort in the New Normal by Kadie Remaklus

Voices of Fibro: The Guidebook for Moms Seeking to Care and Support Their Child Living with Fibromyalgia by Mildred Velez

Ultimate Fulfillment: A Blueprint for Finding and Living Your Purpose by Dr. Joy Kwakuyi

THANK YOU

Thanks for putting this book to use. If you'd like to stay connected, email me through DrJJKelly.com for bonus material. You can also hit me up on Instagram (@DrJJKelly) where there's a ton of free content. There's even more info on my YouTube channel: Dr. JJ Kelly.